BAPTISED
IN THE
SPIRIT?

Other books by John Gunstone

The Feast of Pentecost
Christmas and Epiphany
A Commentary on the New Lectionary (2 vols)
Greater Things than These
The Charismatic Prayer Group
The Beginnings at Whatcombe
A People for His Praise
Pentecostal Anglicans
Live by the Spirit
The Lord is our Healer
Prayers for Healing
Lord Heal Me

BAPTISED
IN THE
SPIRIT?

Fifty questions you wanted to ask

JOHN GUNSTONE

HIGHLAND BOOKS

Cover design: Alison Thomas

ISBN 0 946616 52 3

Printed in Great Britain for
HIGHLAND BOOKS
Broadway House, The Broadway
Crowborough, East Sussex
by Richard Clay Ltd., Bungay, Suffolk
Typeset by Harperset Ltd, Maidstone, Kent.

CONTENTS

CHARISMATIC RENEWAL

BAPTISM IN THE SPIRIT

THE GIFTS OF THE SPIRIT

SPEAKING IN TONGUES, INTERPRETA-
TIONS AND PROPHECIES

GIFTS AND MINISTRIES

GIFTS OF HEALING

RENEWAL IN THE CONGREGATION

INTRODUCTION

Statistics show that the charismatic renewal continues to spread throughout the world and that the
number of Christians whose spiritual lives have
been enriched through it must be in tens of millions.
Yet there is still a good deal of ignorance and
misunderstanding about the renewal among many;
and the situation is not helped when charismatics
assume that everyone else in their congregation
knows what they are talking about when they refer
to baptism in the Spirit or speaking in tongues.

The following fifty questions are the ones that are
asked whenever I have been invited to speak on the
charismatic renewal in Christian gatherings. The
answers are my own. There is no 'official' line
among charismatics about various topics. But I
suspect that many of my friends in the renewal
would agree broadly with what I have written.

Many of the questions require much further
treatment than I have given them here. But I
wanted this to be a short and easy reference book
rather than an extended essay in pastoral theology.
Hopefully those who use it will be led to read
further for themselves when they want to be more
open to the Holy Spirit in their lives.

JOHN GUNSTONE

CHARISMATIC RENEWAL

1. What is the charismatic renewal?

To understand the charismatic renewal, we must first discern how the Holy Spirit renews the church in her first love.

The long story of God's people shows that in every age and in different ways he has to recall them to fresh repentance, faith, and obedience. We read of this often in the old Israel, where the prophets were God's spokesmen: 'Repent! Turn away from all your offences; then sin will not be your downfall. Rid yourselves of all the offences you have committed, and get a new heart and a new spirit,(Ezekiel 18.30-33). It was not enough just to repent; there had to be an interior change and a new beginning in God's strength.

John the Baptist was another agent in God's renewing work when he summoned the people to prepare for the coming of Christ: 'After me will come one more powerful than I, the thongs of whose sandals I am not worthy to stoop down and untie. I baptise you with water, but he will baptise you with the Holy Spirit' (Mark 1. 7-8).

And in the new Israel the apostles had to recall the first congregations to maintain the Christian faith which they had received and to be renewed continually in the Holy Spirit, 'Be joyful always; pray continually; give thanks in all circumstances, for this is God's will for you in Christ Jesus. Do not put out the Spirit's fire' (1 Thessalonians 5.16-19).

It was at such moments that God revealed to the church fresh aspects of the gospel of the kingdom and summoned his people to act in response to what he had revealed. Usually it was individuals or groups who responded first, not the church as a whole. This happened when Peter and those with

him at Caeserea witnessed the descent of the Holy
Spirit on Cornelius and his household and realised
that God was calling Greeks as well as Jews to
repentance, faith and baptism (Acts 10.1-48). Not
everyone in the church agreed with this development. We might say, then, that Peter, Paul and
those who believed 'there is neither Jew nor Greek
in Christ Jesus' (Galatians 3.28) constituted a party
or a 'renewal' within the New Testament church
until what they stood for was generally accepted by
the whole Christian community — a process which
began with the council of the apostles and elders in
Jerusalem (Acts 15.6-29) but which continued far
beyond the New Testament period.

Throughout history many individuals and
groups have risen up for particular causes in the
name of the gospel. Sometimes it is only in
retrospect that we can affirm whether or not they
were truly renewals of the Holy Spirit. Those
involved may be sincerely convinced they are being
led by God, yet in reality they may be misguided.
They need constantly to test their teaching and
practices by submitting them to the scriptures as
reflected on and responded to by Christians
throughout the ages.

God does not contradict himself. If a renewing
movement is not seen to be rooted in the Bible, and
if those who identify themselves with it are not more
Christ-like, then that movement is highly suspect.

Two examples will illustrate what I mean. After
the Black Death in the fourteenth century, groups
of Christian men in various parts of Europe called
people to repentance in order to avert further
plagues which, it was commonly believed, were
signs of divine wrath. These groups organised
public processions in which the men scourged

themselves in penance for their sins and for the sins of others. The flagellants, as they were called, were eventually condemned by the ecclesiastical authorities. Although many of them were sincere in what they did (it is difficult to imagine they would have endured such a painful discipline if they hadn't been), the movement was based on the idea that by punishing ourselves we can atone for our sins. This idea is contrary to the scriptural revelation that only Jesus Christ can take away our sins and that he suffered for them: 'Since we have been justified by his blood, how much more shall we be saved from God's wrath through him' (Romans 5.9).

We can contrast with the flagellants the movement which sprang up in the eighteenth century as a result of the ministry of the Wesley brothers. Although condemned by some Anglicans at the time, John Wesley reached thousands of people with his exposition of the scriptures and his message that the grace of God was what sinners needed and that this grace can produce a spiritual change in those who believe. Charles Wesley's hymns presented this same message in songs which reflected the language of the Bible. The movement was administered through what the Wesleys called 'The Society of People called Methodists', which eventually became a separate denomination. This division — and the further divisions within Methodism itself — were regrettable. But no Christian today would deny that the original impulse which led the Wesleys to initiate their astonishing ministry was a work of the Holy Spirit, a renewing work which began in the Church of England but which was not accepted within it.

During the nineteen-fifties Christians in different parts of the world, reading and praying over their

Bibles, felt dissatisfied because they knew there was a lack of spiritual power in their lives. When they contrasted their own experiences with those of the New Testament church, they realised there were dimensions of the Holy Spirit's work which they had never experienced. They were particularly impressed by the Pentecostal churches which believed that spiritual gifts such as healings, prophecies, tongues and interpretations are still available for the church today. When they began to seek a personal 'baptism in the Holy Spirit' they were astonished to find themselves praying, worshipping, serving and evangelising with a new boldness and authority. They also found themselves led to greater depths of repentance and inner healing.

Since interest was focused on the gift of the Holy Spirit at Pentecost and the manifestations of his gifts, or charisms, this gave the movement the two names by which it is known — 'the new Pentecostal movement' and 'the charismatic movement'. It is often referred to as 'the charismatic renewal' or just 'the renewal', and those who are identified with it as 'charismatics' or (less frequently) 'new Pentecostals'.

What is remarkable about this renewal is that it has spread in every major Christian tradition — Anglican, Baptist, Evangelical, Lutheran, Methodist, Orthodox, Reformed, Roman Catholic. It was reckoned by the end of the nineteen-seventies that about one-tenth of the members of the denominations throughout the world were being influenced by it. Furthermore, it created an experience of unity in Jesus Christ among those who had hitherto been divided for theological, historical and cultural reasons. Although in each mainline denomination the number of charismatics is relatively small, the culminative effect of the renewal has been considerable and there is every sign that it will increase in the future.

2. How did the charismatic renewal start?

It used to be said that the charismatic renewal began on 3 April 1960, when the Rev Dennis Bennett, rector of St Mark's Episcopal Church, Van Nuys, California, announced from the pulpit during the parish eucharist that he had been baptised in the Holy Spirit and spoken in tongues. The story of that incident, and of much that followed from it, is told in his book, *Nine O'Clock in the Morning*. Since it was this experience, reported widely in both the secular and the ecclesiastical media, which made the Christian public aware of what was happening, it is a good starting-point for any popular history of the renewal.

But Peter Hocken, in *Streams of Renewal*, has traced its origins before 1960 in Britain and in the USA. In the early fifties a number of Christian leaders — mostly from Brethren or independent evangelical churches — encountered Pentecostal teaching and were challenged by it. They were led to read the New Testament with fresh insights after meeting those who believed that Christians should experience a personal baptism in the Spirit and that the spiritual gifts of the New Testament, including speaking in tongues, were available for the church today.

This seems to have happened spontaneously at different places in Britain more or less at the same time. In Yorkshire those involved were Cecil Cousen and Philip Rhodes of the Bradford Dean

House Christian Fellowship; in Devon, David Lillie and Arthur Wallis from Brethren circles; in Sussex, Campbell McAlpine and Denis G. Clark.

By 1960 these men had already discovered that they had a common interest in Pentecostal teaching and practices, and they began to organise local conferences to promote what they knew. Cecil Cousen's newsletter, *A Voice of Faith*, with a circulation of 11,000, was widely read.

At the same time in post-war Britain there was a growing interest in the ministry of healing. One of the people closely identified with this was William Wood, an Anglican priest, who in 1949 was appointed warden of the London Healing Mission. Brother Bill, as he was called, also became acquainted in the fifties with Pentecostal teaching about the gift of healing through Donald Gee of the Assemblies of God, and during visits to the USA in 1956 and in 1958. At about this time, too, there were informal prayer groups in a few Anglican parishes who were seeking the gifts of the Spirit.

In the USA there were many individuals and groups outside the Pentecostal churches who were aware of baptism in the Spirit and the spiritual gifts of the New Testament before Dennis Bennett made his famous announcement. I can mention only a few here.

David du Plessis was a Pentecostal leader who in the fifties developed personal contacts with churchmen in the older denominations (a ministry which made him highly suspect in his own). He came to Britain in 1959 to address a series of conferences — the first of many visits to this country and to different parts of the world which he made until he died in 1987. He had a deep appreciation of what he discovered of Jesus Christ in other traditions —

including the Roman Catholic Church (he attended some sessions of the Second Vatican Council). He had a graceful ability to expound from scripture basic Pentecostal teaching in a manner which commanded respect from those who heard him.

The Full Gospel Business Men's Fellowship International, formed in 1951 by Demos Shakarian, a successful Californian dairy-farmer, was a lay organisation set up as a means whereby Pentecostal businessmen could evangelise their friends and acquaintances through prayer breakfasts and conventions, aided by their monthly magazine, *Voice*. They did not seek to integrate into Pentecostal churches those who were baptised in the Spirit at their gatherings, so in this way they contributed indirectly to the increase in the number of charismatics in the older denominations.

Peter Hocken thinks that the person who contributed most to the spread of Pentecostal teaching among those firmly committed to their own church traditions was Agnes Sanford. The wife of an Episcopalian priest, Edgar Sanford, who died in 1960, she developed a healing ministry in the late forties and fifties. In 1953 or 1954 she experienced baptism in the Spirit with the gift of tongues, and from that time onwards she frequently spoke about it in summer schools and conferences for clergy and laity. Through her it spread into the Order of St Luke, an organisation which promotes the healing ministry in the Christian churches in the USA, rather as the London Healing Mission does in Britain.

After 1960 interest in the charismatic renewal spread rapidly in the churches in Britain, the USA, and throughout the Christian world. In Britain Michael Harper resigned from his Anglican curacy in London to set up the Fountain Trust to promote interest in the renewal in Britain through conferences, books and a magazine *(Renewal)*. Similar agencies were established in other countries.

Roman Catholics were involved in the charismatic renewal from the early sixties, but the first to publicise their experiences were a group from the universities of Notre Dame and South Bend in the USA who were baptised in the Spirit in 1967. Their story is told in *Catholic Pentecostals* by Kevin and Dorothy Ranaghan, where the experience was interpreted as a fulfilment of Pope John XXIII's prayer for a 'new Pentecost' in the Roman Catholic Church. *Catholic Pentecostals* was as influential among members of that church as *Nine O'Clock in the Morning* was among Anglicans and Protestants. The renewal spread rapidly among Roman Catholics throughout the world.

This, then, was the first phase. The second phase began when Roman Catholics began setting up their own service agencies in each country and an international communications centre in Rome to promote the renewal. That policy was copied by charismatics in other denominations as they sought to apply the lessons of the renewal to their own fellowships and structures.

3. What are the distinctive features of the charismatic renewal?

1. Belief that the Holy Spirit in his fulness is available for all those who have repented of their sins and who have accepted Jesus Christ as their Saviour and Lord.

This is, of course, orthodox Christian teaching, but the charismatic renewal has given this particular article of the creed ('I believe in the Holy

Spirit') a new emphasis.

Charismatics claim that to receive this fulness we must be baptised in, with or by, the Holy Spirit. Many Christians receive this 'Spirit baptism', as it is called, after they have been baptised in water — years afterwards in the case of those who were christened in infancy. The New Testament pattern is that we should be baptised in water and in the Spirit more or less at the same time. But this is rare, except when an individual is converted and prepared for believer's baptism in the expectation that 'Spirit baptism' will be received during the administration of the sacrament.

2. *Belief that the gifts of the Holy Spirit, as revealed in the New Testament, are available for equipping the Christian and the church in every age, including our own.*

One consequence of this belief is that charismatics look for a wider spectrum of spiritual gifts than many other Christians. If we assume that we can catalogue all the gifts of the Spirit under the letters A to Z (the charisms, of course, cannot be limited in this way, but for the purposes of this illustration we will assume they can), then the charisms A to P are those spiritual gifts which are expected in most congregations — leadership, evangelism, giving generously to those in need, teaching, pastoral care, keeping the financial accounts, music, and so on. The charisms Q to Z, however, are those spiritual gifts which have not been expected so often — such as prophecy, healings, speaking in tongues and interpretations of tongues.

3. *Expectation that the Lord's guidance and power will be experienced as we submit every part of our lives to him.*

Although charismatics are not shielded from the doubts, weaknesses and temptations which assail all of us — the evil one seems to single out those

whom the Spirit touches for special attention —
they have a lively awareness of Jesus Christ's
presence and lordship in everyday things. They
tend to speak of him with a directness which some
other Christians find disconcerting. Phrases such as
'the Lord told me' or 'the Holy Spirit led me' reflect
this expectation.

The practice has led to the criticism that charismatics think they have a 'hot line to God'.
Perhaps some charismatics are misguided enough
to believe that. But most of them, when they use
such phrases, are expressing their trust that God is
involved in all that they say or do. They would be
more accurate (and would avoid much misunderstanding) if they said '*I believe* the Lord told me' or
'*it seemed* the Holy Spirit led me'.

*4. Response to the Bible as a revelation of the word of
God.*

Among charismatics are many who have been
brought up in the critical, questioning approach to
the scriptures characteristic of contemporary biblical theology. When they are baptised in the Holy
Spirit, they find that the Bible acquires a greater
authority and a relevance than they had discerned
before.

To dismiss this as a form of neo-fundamentalism
(which accepts the scriptures as true in historical
and scientific detail) is to misunderstand the nature
of this response. Generally speaking, charismatics
do not abandon what they have learned through
their biblical study, but they reassess their understanding of it as a consequence of what they discern
through their new experiences of God's grace. For
example, the stories of healings in the Bible are seen
in a different light when a healing has been
experienced in their own lives.

5. Worship with an emphasis on joyful praise and thanksgiving.

The charismatic renewal has been accompanied by a prolific outpouring of new songs and choruses, mostly inspired by biblical themes. This kind of worship springs from a profound awareness of God's love in Jesus Christ and an uplifting of heart and mind by the Holy Spirit.

When we are renewed by the Holy Spirit, then the material for worship he has given to God's people in the past — the psalms, the canticles of the Old and New Testaments, traditional liturgical material in prayer books and the songs of praise in hymn books — comes alive in a fresh way. Among charismatic groups and congregations generally there has been a deeper appreciation of both liturgical and spontaneous prayer. Those evangelicals who have regarded set prayers as 'unspiritual', and those traditionalists who have dismissed free prayer as 'subjective', have learned to appreciate what is of the Spirit in their different practices.

6. Experiences of oneness in Jesus Christ which overarches denominational and theological barriers.

Charismatics are given a powerful sense of union with Christians. For example, a charismatic evangelical often discovers a deeper unity with a charismatic Roman Catholic than he would previously have imagined possible.

The divisions caused by doctrinal and other differences are still real, of course, but charismatics who try to be obedient to the Spirit are also aware of the things which unite them in the Lord. As a result the charismatic renewal has given an impetus to ecumenical endeavours at local as well as national levels. The breaking down of long-standing hostile barriers between Catholics and

Protestants in Ireland, for example, has been little less than miraculous.

One of the most popular choruses sung by charismatics is

We are one in the Spirit, we are one in the Lord,
and we pray that all unity will one day be restored,
and they'll know we are Christians by our love.

7. *Recognition of an every-member ministry as the mainspring for the church's life and mission.*

Charismatics have a vision of the Body of Christ in which each believer receives spiritual gifts so that he or she may fulfil his or her own role in the church. Often this results in the formation of communities of believers linked together formally or informally in mutual commitment. In the sermons of the renewal the church is presented as the herald of God's kingdom, confronting evil and proclaiming righteousness.

Charismatics are criticised for being more concerned with their spiritual growth than with their involvement in social and political issues. They are also accused of talking more about evangelism than doing it. No doubt such criticisms are just in many cases — baptism in the Spirit does not instantly equip us to be ardent campaigners for human rights or persuasive preachers of the good news. But individuals, groups and congregations often find themselves being led in the name of the Lord into forms of service and outreach that they had not imagined before.

8. *Awareness of spiritual warfare.*

Charismatics sense the inner-battle warfare in which Christians are involved. Evil as an objective power challenging the authority and goodness of God is very real in their experience.

As we become more aware of the Holy Spirit, so we become more aware of unholy spirits. The phrase in the Lord's Prayer, 'Deliver us from evil', takes on a new significance.

Other Christians, influenced by our secularised culture, find this aspect of the charismatic renewal difficult to accept. They are not helped by the fact that, in the early days of the renewal, some of its leaders so stressed the demonic that their hearers were tempted to attribute all their sins, weaknesses and misfortunes to evil spirits. A more balanced view is now widespread, which accepts that the New Testament view of evil must be taken seriously and which also recognises that not everything wrong in the individual and in society can be explained exclusively in psychological and sociological terms.

Obviously some, if not all, of these features of the charismatic renewal I have listed can be detected in other Christian renewals as well. It is not only charismatics who respond to the Bible as the revelation of the word of God, and it is not only charismatics who are concerned that every member of a Christian congregation should exercise his or her God-given ministry. But what is distinctive about the charismatic renewal is that it has brought these characteristics together and given them a high profile in the church's teaching and practice of Christian discipleship.

4. Why do some Christians say the charismatic renewal is unscriptural?

The accusation comes from those who regard the teaching of the renewal to have deviated from the Bible as they interpret it. Such Christians are

generally very sincere in what they say, and their
concern is not so much to score points in a
theological argument as to ensure that the truth of
the gospel is not obscured. Charismatics should
treat this accusation gently and do all they can to
continue the discussion, so that both they and those
who criticise them seek to understand more fully
what God requires of us.

Briefly, criticism of the renewal usually revolves
round two arguments.

(1) There is no evidence that the New Testament
promises a 'second blessing' following the initial
forgiveness and incorporation into Jesus Christ
through repentance, faith and baptism. When
charismatics urge born-again believers to be baptised in the Spirit, say these critics, they are urging
us to an experience which is false. What is called
'being baptised in the Holy Spirit' is the initial and
initiating endowment of the indwelling Spirit,
which Christ as Lord gives to all whom he makes,
and marks as, his own. All those who have come to
Christ have, then, already been baptised in the
Spirit, and to seek another and subsequent experience of 'Spirit baptism' is erroneous. Believers are
not divided into two classes — those who are
baptised in the Spirit and those who are not. We are
all one in Christ, for 'if anyone does not have the
Spirit of Christ, he does not belong to Christ'
(Romans 8.9).

Furthermore, what charismatics call baptism in
the Spirit often seems to stem from a desire for
emotional experiences which at their best are not
basic to our Christian calling and at their worst are
positively dangerous.

(2) Claims that the spiritual gifts described in the
New Testament are available for today are mislead-

ing. Charisms such as tongues and healings were only manifested in the apostolic church as a special dispensation from God in the early days of the gospel. Once that age was past and the church's mission was established, these gifts were withdrawn. God now provides other means of bearing witness to the power of his Word and healing grace. What passes for speaking in tongues is a self-generated form of expression, and what are described as gifts of healing are rapid forms of recovery which may well have medical or psychological explanations.

Looking at these two criticisms, we have to admit that there is some justification for the first. Although the renewal was not entirely dependent on the teaching and practices of the Pentecostal churches, it did nevertheless learn a good deal from them. Early teachers in the renewal repeated the classic Pentecostal doctrine that after conversion there is a second encounter with God in which the Christian receives the supernatural power of the Holy Spirit into his life. This Pentecostals call a second 'baptism' a second 'experience', a second 'blessing'.

Later teachers modified this and explained that baptism in the Spirit is an individual's greater yielding to or receiving of the Spirit. Nevertheless the impression can be given that charismatics are claiming a 'second blessing' when they urge their Christian friends to be baptised in the Spirit. It is not easy to explain that God has much more for us without seeming to imply that, if you don't accept that, you're second-best!

Having said that, however, the baptism in the Spirit experience opens up areas of Christian devotion and ministry which many have never realised before. And, although charismatics do not want to divide Christians into two classes, it often seems that, as far as they are concerned personally, their Christian expectation before their baptism in the Spirit experience was a pale shadow of what it became afterwards.

There is less justification for the second criticism. The concept of a two-stage Christian history is illogical if it is applied over the centuries. If Jesus Christ is the same yesterday, today and for ever, why should he act differently in the apostolic age than in subsequent ages? Where is the scriptural evidence for such 'dispensationalism', as this view is called?

What is called speaking in tongues may some-times be nothing more than self-generated express-ion; but at other times glossolalia can be a means of building up an individual's faith or of conveying (through an interpretation) a word from the Lord. On such occasions the speaking in tongues man-ifested in charismatic gatherings seems very close to what was experienced in New Testament times.

Furthermore, as the ministry of healing is exer-cised more widely in different churches, physical and other healings are experienced in remarkable ways. These do not contradict the many gifts which come through skilful medical and nursing care, but they provide another dimension to what it means in Christian terms to be 'made whole'.

The criticism that the renewal is unscriptural is not justified if we read our Bible in the light of what is experienced when the renewal is faithful to the loving work of the Spirit. There is certainly need for more theological reflection on the renewal, so that we are helped to discern what in it is genuine and what are its cultural accretions. But if charismatics

are becoming more aware of God as their Father
and Jesus Christ as their Lord and Saviour through
the renewal, it is difficult to see how they can be
accused of deviating from God's revelation of
himself in the Bible.

5. Why is the charismatic renewal so divisive?

Some congregations have experienced divisions as a
result of becoming involved in charismatic renewal.
In a few places — usually in local churches of a
strong independent evangelical character — there
has been a sizeable breakaway, with perhaps up to
half of the total membership walking out and
forming another church. In other places — usually
in the more traditional denominations — the
division has not been so marked: individuals and
small groups have drifted away into what they
perceive as 'more Spirit-filled' congregations. The
growth of the house church movement owes much
to these tendencies.

   The sad thing about these divisions has been the
sense of rejection and bitterness which has accompanied them. Nothing weakens the worship and
witness of a congregation more than the spectacle of
its members fighting one another. The seeds of
discord bear a sour fruit. That became evident even
in New Testament times. Such a situation in
Corinth, for example, drew a stern rebuke from
Paul.

   At the beginning of his letter to the congregation
he thanked God that 'you have been enriched in
every way...(and) you do not lack any spiritual gift
as you eagerly wait for our Lord Jesus Christ to be
revealed' (1 Corinthians 1.5-7). Yet at the same
time he took them to task because of quarrels

arising from their party spirit: 'One of you says, "I follow Paul"; another, "I follow Apollos"; another, "I follow Cephas"; still another, "I follow Christ"' (1 Corinthians 1.12). Their fellowship was fractured by a partisanship which resulted from over-emphasising differences among the various apostles in their teaching.

The divisions which happen nowadays do not stem so much from allegiance to individual leaders as from commitment to different emphases. The causes of disagreements are a mixture of personal and temperament differences as well as doctrinal and cultural ones.

Traditionalists, with a strong sense of what they owe to the past, want to preserve the things they are familiar with, like the historic or authorised liturgies of the church, and 'the way we've always done it'. They often resist practices which are associated with the renewal, such as new and enthusiastic styles of music, or clapping and the raising of hands during prayer.

Evangelical church members highly value those theological convictions which are based on the authority and inspiration of the scriptures, generally interpreted from a Protestant viewpoint. They emphasise personal and group Bible study, personal evangelism and missionary concern. Some interpretations of biblical passages, such as the affirmation that Jesus Christ baptises us in his Spirit or heals the sick through spiritual gifts now, disturbs them.

Liberal church members are more questioning in their approach to the Christian revelation. They are prepared to debate issues that are raised by traditional doctrines, and they are inclined to relate Christian faith and practice to contemporary philosophies and psychologies as they attempt to reach out to modern men and women. To them some of the teaching and expectations of the renewal appear naive. They stress that faith must result in good works if it is to be true to Jesus Christ. Consequently they throw their energies into social and political involvement of all kinds, from projects related to world development and nuclear disarmament to schemes for changing government policies and aiding the underprivileged in our society. They regard a stress on personal spiritual growth as inward-looking.

Charismatics are not always wise in the manner they approach the rest of the congregation. Often they give the impression that they are in direct contact with Almighty God in every situation and that for them the only true worship is that which involves choruses, spontaneity, and singing in the Spirit.

Unfortunately the labels I have used can divide Christians as well as describe them, when the things they emphasise become the focus of attention. Preference turns into partisanship, factions appear, and divisions do their deadly work. Paul asked the Corinthians, 'Is Christ divided? Was Paul crucified for you?' (1 Corinthians 1.13). Today we might ask, 'Did your traditional practices, your evangelical theology, your liberal interpretations, or your charismatic involvement give you new life in Christ?'

How should we try and solve these divisions when they arise? How can we help to bring healing to a congregation?

1. We should affirm that we are not looking for an imposed uniformity. There should be no suggestion that we expect those who don't see things our way to get out. That would be turning the Christian

congregation into a sect, which exercises an authority that does not allow any significant differences among its adherents. A sect says to its members, 'Either come with us our way, or get out.' In contrast, a Christian congregation is a community, and a genuine community welcomes diversity of expression in the worship and service of its Lord. Indeed, the biblical understanding of a Christian community is that it contains a diversity of gifts and ministry united in Jesus Christ and bound together by his love.

2. We should reject negotiated solutions which attempt to find a political compromise. Church leaders and outside consultants often take this route, seeking a compromise in which everyone feels they have scored at least some points. The result is that differences are not brought out into the open, discussed and prayed over, and the congregation is expected to assent to a compromise which satisfies no one.

3. We should gently remind everyone concerned that the scriptural way to reconciliation and unity lies through confession of sins and genuine repentance. Party spirit and factions — so easily copied from what goes on in the political world (local as well as national) — are symptoms of pride, selfishness, and a desire to control. These must die if the body of Christ is to be healthy. And that process begins when we start saying sorry to one another and asking one another for forgiveness.

4. We should together seek the Lord's guidance so that we can discern how differences among us reflect the Holy Spirit's gifts and ministries. Then we can begin to plan together how the different gifts and ministries are to be exercised for the glory of God and for the building up of the church. We shall

discover that it is not the things which are at issue which divide (traditional worship, evangelism, social concern, speaking in tongues) so much as the individuals and groups who make them occasions for division.

On the night of his betrayal, Jesus said to his disciples: 'All will know that you are my disciples if you love one another.... Love each other as I have loved you' (John 13.35; 15.12). About twenty-five years later Paul wrote to the congregation at Corinth: 'This love of which I speak is slow to lose patience — it looks for a way of being constructive. It is not possessive; it is neither anxious to impress nor does it cherish inflated ideas of its own importance' (1 Corinthians 13.4, J.B. Phillips' paraphrase).

Augustine, Bishop of Hippo (d. 430), said a wise word about preventing divisions and fostering a Spirit-filled community: 'In essentials, unity; in non-essentials, diversity; in all things, love.'

6. How widespread is the charismatic renewal?

The term 'charismatic renewal' is used to describe a variety of different Christian movements in the twentieth century, so in order to assemble a complete picture, we need to distinguish these movements. They are as follows:

1. Classical Pentecostal movement

These groups owe their origins to the teaching of Charles Fox Parham (Topeka, 1901) and William J. Seymour (Los Angeles, 1906). What distinguishes them from other charismatics is the acceptance of what is called 'the initial evidence' theory. This holds that speaking in tongues is the necessary first evidence of receiving the 'baptism in the Holy

Spirit'. Although these groups differ among themselves in questions concerning the nature of God,
sanctification and divine healing, they represent
one historic stream of Christianity in most nations
of the world. In Britain they are represented by
such churches as the Assemblies of God and the
Elim Pentecostal. In the *World Christian Encyclopedia*
David B. Barrett gives the following statistics:

1970:	36,794,000
1980:	51,167,200
1985:	58,999,900

2. *Mainline Protestant charismatics*

The charismatic renewal in the mainline Protestant churches began in the fifties and sixties. At
first those involved were called 'neo-Pentecostals'.
These neo-Pentecostals differed from their prede-
cessors in that they seldom subscribed to the 'initial
evidence' theory and that they practised a more
restrained form of worship than their more demon-
strative Pentecostal counterparts. They were generally also from a higher socio-economic level and
their leaders more academic. Those in liturgical
and sacramental churches saw baptism in the Spirit
more in terms of spiritual growth than second
blessing.

Anglicans:	1975:	109,900
	1980:	1,090,200
	1985:	1,660,800
Protestants:	1975:	824,100
	1980:	2,112,700
	1985:	4,286,800

3. The Catholic charismatics

Beginning in the USA in the sixties, the Catholic charismatic renewal developed rapidly and spread to other parts of the world in the next two decades. From the beginning the renewal grew under the generally benevolent scrutiny of the hierarchy and was studied by theologians and sociologists.

The Protestant and Catholic renewals developed along similar paths, both borrowing from and contributing to each other. Yet, although commended by Pope Paul IV, the renewal has not succeeded in making much impact on the pastoral structures of the Roman Catholic Church, compared with the Anglican Church. In the latter it has been the main force behind such developments as lay eldership, the healing ministry, and evangelism. Catholics have developed the healing ministry, especially with the use of anointing by laity as well as clergy (for which provision is made in their liturgical rites); but lay eldership and evangelism are still rare.

4. The house churches

As Pentecostalism developed, it produced many independent groupings which were not organically connected with these earlier expressions of the renewal. The outstanding ministries of individual leaders has led to a proliferation of new groupings centering round magnetic personalities and variant teachings that have not always been accepted by the major denominations.

This is the origin of 'the house churches' — so called because they often began when a few individuals broke away from a denominational church to worship in their own homes and gradually attracted followers. The name has remained

even though some of these groups now possess
church buildings and have established a denomina-
tion-like network of relationships among themselves. In England the 'Restoration' or 'Abundant
Life' Christian fellowships constitute one of the
largest of these. No serious survey of them has
produced any figures, but the impression is that in
Britain, at any rate, their membership will have
grown to the half-a-million mark by the end of the
eighties.

5. *Third World indigenous groups*

The fastest-growing Pentecostal movements in
the world are not directly related to the above
groups. Rather, they consist of indigenous movements independent of western missionary societies.
Some of these observe orthodox Protestant worship
and theological forms; others can be classified as
only semi-Christian. Although classical Pentecostal
bodies often deny any relationship with them, these
groups are usually assigned to the Pentecostal
family because they do not easily fit into any other
category. The Zionist Apostolic movement in South
Africa with over three million members is one
example. Again, it is difficult to find any reliable
statistics.

6. *Orthodox charismatics*

Recent years have seen the emergence of charismatic renewal in churches of the Orthodox
tradition. It is found not only among those churches
whose congregations are in the West (especially in
the USA) but also among their congregations in the
East. There is a significant movement, for example,
among the Orthodox in the USSR and among the
Copts in Egypt.

Orthodox: 1975:   15,200
             1980:   157,000
             1985:   241,000

When we try to assess how widespread the
charismatic renewal is among the denominations, it
has to be said that identification is becoming more
difficult. Twenty years ago charismatics could be
singled out as those who claimed they had had an
experience of a Pentecostal baptism in the Spirit
and who frequented charismatic prayer groups,
rallies and conferences. Now the distinctive lessons
of the charismatic renewal are being accepted so
widely that many who have not been to charismatic
gatherings and who do not think of themselves as
charismatics are nevertheless being deeply influenced by the renewal.

A distinguished evangelical asked an Anglican
clergyman if the services in his church were charismatic.

The clergyman considered the question for a
moment.

'Charismatic-ish,' he replied cautiously.

The evangelical smiled.

'Aren't we all a bit '-ish these days?' he said.

BAPTISM IN THE SPIRIT

7. What is 'baptism in the Spirit'?

During the forty days in which the risen Christ was with his disciples, speaking about the kingdom of God, he told them, 'Do not leave Jerusalem, but wait for the gift my Father promised, which you have heard me speak about. For John baptised with water, but in a few days you will be baptised with the Holy Spirit' (Acts 1.5).

His instructions, and the subsequent outpouring of the Holy Spirit on his disciples on the day of Pentecost, fulfilled the prophecies of the Old Testament and of John the Baptist. Joel had foretold that the day of the Lord would be one when the Holy Spirit of God would be manifested in a new way ('I will pour out my Spirit on all people' — Joel 2.28), and John had told the people to expect the coming of one who would baptise them with the Holy Spirit (Matthew 3.11; Mark 1.8; Luke 3.16). The fourth evangelist called Jesus 'the Baptiser in Holy Spirit' (John 1.33: the Greek reads, 'the one baptising in Holy Spirit').

The Greek *baptizein* means to dip, to immerse, to plunge under water. To be baptised in the Spirit, then, is a metaphorical way of saying we are immersed in the Spirit, as an adult candidate for baptism is immersed in water. We mean being inundated by, submerged in, or pervaded with the presence and power of God. Other terms used in the New Testament are: 'filled with the Spirit' (Acts 2.4, 9.17; Ephesians 5.18), 'pouring out of the Spirit'(Acts 2.17), 'receiving the Spirit' (Acts 2.38, 8.15, 19.2; Galatians 3.2), and 'sealed with the Spirit' (Ephesians 1.13).

The water metaphor for the Spirit of God goes back to the Old Testament. To receive God's blessing is like receiving rain in a dry land. Water stands for divine presence and power: 'With joy you will draw water from the wells of salvation' (Isaiah 12.3; *cf*. Ezekiel 47.1 and Zechariah 4.10). Those who obey God are 'like a well-watered garden, like a spring whose waters never fail' (Isaiah 58.11). The analogy between the work of the Holy Spirit in the believer and the role of water in giving life was taken up by Jesus. He told the woman at the well in Samaria that she should ask God for the 'living water' (John 4.10), and he proclaimed in Jerusalem on the last day of the feast, 'if anyone is thirsty, let him come to me and drink. Whosoever believes in me, as the scripture has said, streams of living water will flow from within him' (John 7.37-38). Linked with this is the use of water in Christian initiation as a sign of cleansing from sin, dying and rising with Christ, and admission to the community of faith — all the work of the Spirit.

When charismatics say they have experienced 'baptism in the Spirit', they mean that what the risen Christ did at the first Pentecost is becoming a greater reality in their lives. Either suddenly or gradually over a period of time, they become more aware than before that the gospel of Jesus Christ challenges them in all they think, do and say. They are conscious of a new outpouring of the Spirit into their lives. They are convicted of their sins — but they also sense the forgiveness which Jesus brings through the cross, and the love that the Father has for them and for others. They desire to be more faithful disciples of Christ and they hope to receive more power to serve him.

However, there are many misunderstandings around about this experience, so perhaps it will be helpful to explain what baptism in the Spirit is *not*:

1. It is not something in which we are so possessed by God that we lose our personal identities.

We are not coerced by divine power. What happens is that, because we want to be more open to the Spirit, he begins to energise us in such a way that we gradually realise we are being given new possibilities and previously unknown capabilities. The Spirit of God blows upon our human spirits to release us into a fuller freedom in Jesus Christ.

2. It is not a promotion from being a second-class into a first-class Christian.

Some are tempted to believe that, because they are indwelt by the Spirit, they have a gift of instant sanctification. Teachings about perfectionism have hung around the charismatic renewal, relics of the nineteenth-century holiness movements from which the Pentecostal churches sprang. But you only have to make friends with a few charismatics — or, better still, live with them — to discover they are by no means perfect. Hopefully those who are baptised in the Spirit will become more Christ-like, and certainly over a period of time their friends should see signs of the Spirit's work in changing them. But baptism in the Spirit has more to do with penetration of life rather than with holiness of character.

3. It is not an initiation into a spirit-trip to make us feel good.

Being baptised in the Spirit can be an emotional experience for many Christians. When they receive prayer with the laying on of hands for baptism in the Spirit, some experience a sense of release which causes them to laugh with joy or weep with thankfulness. Increasing awareness of the immensity of God's love can cause deep emotions. But baptism in the Spirit doesn't focus our attention on the Holy Spirit; the third person of the

Trinity points us to Jesus Christ as our Lord and
Saviour. He is the one who 'baptises with the Holy
Spirit'. However much we may be moved emotionally, or however much we may be fascinated by
certain charisms (speaking in tongues, healing), the
ultimate result of Spirit baptism is growth into a
closer and more faithful relationship with God
through Jesus Christ. If this is not the result, then
we have not been baptised in the Spirit.

4. It is not the same as conversion.

In every case that I have known, the individual
seeking to be baptised in the Spirit already had
some faith in Jesus Christ. Many of them afterwards looked back and felt that their previous life of
faith had been inadequate. Even those who had
dramatic personal conversion experiences said that
baptism in the Spirit opened up for them further
understandings of what their conversion entailed.
Evangelicals who have seen conversion in terms of
commitment to Jesus Christ and the word of God in
the scriptures have had their vision widened to
include personal commitment to the Christian
community. Catholics who have seen conversion in
terms of faithful churchmanship and reception of
the sacraments have had their vision widened to
include personal commitment to Jesus Christ in the
scriptures. And so on.

5. It is not a once-for-all event.

Although the initial baptism in the Spirit is often
a memorable experience, and charismatics usually
refer to it as such, it is essentially a continuing
immersion in the love and power of God. 'Since we
live by the Spirit, let us keep in step with the Spirit'
is how Paul described it (Gal.5.25). It is not usual
to speak of 'new baptism in the Spirit', but we will
need to seek the Lord afresh each day and ask him

to plunge us into his Spirit again in preparation for what he sends us to do.

6. *It is not initiation into speaking in tongues.*

In the teaching charismatics have inherited from Pentecostal spirituality, baptism in the Holy Spirit is closely associated with speaking in tongues. Quite often this particular charism will be given when we ask the Lord to baptise us in his Spirit, or shortly afterwards. It can be an encouraging sign that the Lord is at work within us. But it is not essential. We should resist the idea that if we do not speak in tongues we have not received the Spirit. There are good reasons why this spiritual gift is widespread today, but there are no New Testament grounds for believing that speaking in tongues is always an authentic and essential accompaniment to being baptised in the Spirit.

7. *It is not a second baptism.*

For Christians there is only one baptism (Ephesians 4.5) because there is only one initiation into Christ (Romans 6.1-4). As we have seen above, baptism in the Spirit is a metaphorical way of expressing the Spirit's coming, just as the phrase 'to be baptised' was used metaphorically to refer to Jesus' death and resurrection (Mark 10.39 and parallels). 'A new sending of the Spirit' is a good description of baptism in the Spirit. It shows that baptism in the Spirit is not just a metaphorical description of an experience but also a theological truth. It also associates baptism in the Spirit with other 'sendings' of the Spirit which we expect when, for example, we pray with the laying on of hands for someone to be commissioned for particular work in the church, such as being ordained, or when we pray for people who are moving into a different state of life, such as getting married. In this

connection it is noteworthy that after Peter and
John had been released by the Sanhedrin, they and
the other disciples were all filled afresh with the
Holy Spirit as on the day of Pentecost (Acts 4.31).

*8. It is not something invoked by fervent prayer and inner
excitement.*

Baptism in the Spirit is a sovereign act of God,
not just a change in our subjective consciousness.
Through a fresh sending of the Spirit (often as a
result of our petitions and the prayers of others) we
become more conscious of the power of God
because the Spirit is at work in us in a new way. If
he is present in us in a new way, that is because he
has been sent from the Father and through the Son,
who is the Baptiser in the Spirit.

Some plead that we should stop using the phrase
'baptism in the Spirit'. They point out that it causes
misunderstandings such as those I have just listed.
Others, however, feel that until all Christians are
taught to expect the empowering of Pentecost, we
need this phrase to emphasise the lesson. Whether
we call the experience baptism in the Spirit or
something else, what is vital is that we should
always be completely open to the Spirit of God in
our lives.

8. How were you baptised in the Spirit?

It was in the spring of 1964 that the telephone rang
in the small house which served as a vicarage of the
Romford parish where I was then priest-in-charge.

'Hello?' I said, picking up the receiver.

'You may not remember me — I'm Marion. We
met in Mersea some months ago.'

I remembered her. She was a deaconess in a
London parish, but her home was on Mersea Island

near Colchester, Essex, where a friend, Reg East, was vicar.

'Yes?'

Her next question took me completely by surprise.

'What do you know about speaking in tongues?'

In those days that was the last thing I expected anyone to ask me over the phone. Also, there was a note of anxiety in her voice which made me feel uneasy.

I struggled to recall the references to glossolalia I had half-noticed in the New Testament.

'I don't think St Paul was too keen on it,' I replied cautiously.

'But Reg's in the thick of it down in Mersea,' she went on. 'Everybody's talking about it. I'm worried about him.'

I was mystified.

'What's he been doing?'

'I don't know any details, but I don't like the sound of it. I rang you because I thought you might be able to help him out of it.'

After she had rung off, I thumbed through the references to speaking in tongues in the Bible and wondered how Reg could have become involved in such a practice. I knew Pentecostals spoke in tongues, but that was a whole Atlantic away from what I expected in the Church of England.

I had known Reg East since my college days. He had a heart-warming faith in God and an enthusiasm for his work as an Anglican parish priest which I admired. It certainly wasn't like him to get involved in the weird goings-on of what I then thought of as fringe Christian groups.

After pondering the matter for a few days, I decided the most tactful thing to do would be to

write to him. I composed an inconsequential letter
about nothing in particular, but at the end mentioned casually that I had heard that he had been
speaking in tongues and said I hoped it improved
his mastery of foreign languages.

Back came his reply a few days later. He said that
he and his wife, Lucia, were learning what remarkable things God was doing in the church and they
were trying to be led by the Holy Spirit themselves.

The next few weeks took me through a series of
events which seemed later to have been following a
carefully-laid plan. I might have called them
'coincidences' once. Now I would call them 'God-
incidences'.

First, I went down to Mersea and learned from
Reg and Lucia how they had been sent a magazine
called *Trinity* produced in California with stories of
how Christians in different churches were redis-
covering the power of the Holy Spirit in their daily
lives. Speaking in tongues, interpretations, prophecies, healings, spiritual gifts of all kinds — it was as
if the apostolic age was being revived all over again.

I learned, too, that Reg had received the laying
on of hands from two young Pentecostal ministers
and had begun to speak in tongues when he prayed.
Lucia had received the gift a few days' later. They
said they had never known the vitality of the
Christian faith in such a way before — and, looking
at them, I could believe that. I felt mildly envious of
their obvious joy and confidence in the Lord.

Next, I was invited, as a member of the editorial
committee of our diocesan paper, to a press
conference at the Savoy Hotel in London to meet a
Mrs Jean Stone, the editor of *Trinity*. Forty or so
people crowded into the Gondoliers Room with its
heavy red decor — a fantastic setting for the story

we heard. Mrs Stone spoke to us with poise and assurance: Dennis Bennett, her Episcopalian parish priest, had received the baptism in the Holy Spirit along with many of his parishioners, and they had launched *Trinity* to spread the news of what was happening to them.

After the conference I cornered the organiser, a curate of All Souls, Langham Place, and asked him to give me a demonstration of speaking in tongues. He closed his eyes and whispered in a strange language. It was uncanny. When he finished, Michael Harper told me he was leaving All Souls to establish a body called the Fountain Trust, which would promote interest in the charismatic renewal in England. He was organising a conference on spiritual gifts at Stoke Poges in a week's time and he had one spare place. Would I like to come?

So that led to the third 'God-incidence'. I attended the conference with a group of clergy and ministers from different denominations to listen to David du Plessis, a former secretary of the Pentecostal World Conference, as he expounded the work of the Holy Spirit in the church. He had been attending the Second Vatican Council as an observer, and through what he said about conversations he had had with Roman Catholic bishops and theologians, I realised how little I had known about the charismatic nature of the Body of Christ.

Contrary to what I had imagined, the apostolic age of the church is not passed. By the one Spirit we are still living in it! I was thrilled. Over and over again I kept asking myself, Why hadn't I seen this before? There this truth was, calling to me out of the pages of the New Testament, expounded by the graceful Pentecostal teacher. It was as a result of listening to David du Plessis that my curiosity

about the charismatic renewal was converted into a
desire to receive the Holy Spirit more fully into my
life. I was not clear what that meant, but I knew I
wanted it.

The fourth and final 'God-incidence' was when I
went back to Mersea and asked Reg East to pray
with me that I might be baptised in the Holy Spirit.
We were in the lounge of his vicarage. We sat facing
one another, and he prayed that the Lord would
give me all that God desired I should have. Then he
stood behind my chair and laid his hands on me,
speaking in a strange tongue as he did so — an
oriental-sounding language, beautiful in its
cadences and consonants.

I opened my mouth hopefully and made a few
sounds, but nothing happened that persuaded me I
was speaking in tongues.

'It's no good, Reg,' I said at last.

He returned to his chair, looking nonplussed. I
discovered afterwards that he had never laid hands
on anyone for baptism in the Spirit before, and he
had no idea what he should do next. Eventually he
suggested that I prayed for a renewal in the Spirit
again when I was alone; and I returned home
feeling perplexed and unworthy.

I prayed again a few days later. I was kneeling
alone in the church in Romford, gazing at the
figures of Christ on the cross, the Virgin Mary and
St John on the east wall. Suddenly I sensed an
overshadowing of God's love such as I had rarely
experienced before. I felt rising within me a longing
to praise the Lord with the whole of my being.

The joy of it was overwhelming. I wanted to
laugh, cry, sing, all at the same time. Then words
came tumbling out in a gift of tongues, and I felt I
was rejoicing in the forgiveness and love and

goodness of God in a new way.

Looking back on those 'God-incidences' after a quarter of a century or so, it strikes me how, through my encounter with charismatic renewal, God rescued me from my bleak encounter with the radical theological questioning of the sixties.

Those years had brought me to the point where I began to doubt whether or not there was a God to believe in. If God was 'out there' (to use what was then the fashionable phrase), then he was a very long way off out there. In fact, I might have believed 'God was dead' (another fashionable phrase).

Through what I experienced in 1964 I started daring to believe once more — to believe that God could take control of my life and the lives of others, if we were prepared to take risks in letting him do this.

Teaching on spiritual gifts gave me the scriptural and theological undergirding for taking these risks. Although there is a lot of me that doesn't want to trust God completely — I still want to ask questions and I still feel doubts — yet deep down I know God 'is able to do immeasurably more than all we ask or imagine, according to his power that is at work within us' (Ephesians 3.20).

That is what baptism in the Holy Spirit means to me. It doesn't make me a first-class Christian. Far from it. (Ask anyone who knows me well.) But it has made me realise that 'normal Christianity' is more intimately linked with what I read about in the New Testament than I had previously expected.

Many other Christians, I am sure, have got onto that gospel track without ever having heard of the charismatic renewal or without speaking in tongues. The Holy Spirit works in many different

ways. But that is the way he worked in bringing me
to where I am now, and I praise him for it as I tell
my story.

9. How can I be baptised in the Spirit?

You ask Jesus Christ to baptise you in the Holy
Spirit and then believe that he has responded to
your request. And for people whose faith is sincere
and uncomplicated, that is how they are renewed in
the Spirit. But most of us are not as sincere as that.
Because we complicate our lives by sins and doubts
and fears, we need help from others.

When someone asks me to pray with them for
Spirit-baptism, I first see if there is another
Christian whom I can invite to join me in prayer
with them. In many forms of ministry or service,
two are better than one.

Then I usually go through the following programme:

1. I pray aloud for the guidance of the Spirit, and
I encourage the one I am praying with to do the
same.

2. I ask him if he has committed himself to Jesus
Christ as his Saviour and Lord. If he says something like, 'I'm a regular church-goer,' I put a
further question to see if his shyness in mentioning
the name of Jesus is just unfamiliarity with this kind
of 'evangelical' language, or if it is symptomatic of a
personal difficulty. Some people who have been
influenced by evil cannot use the divine name
without showing distress (see 3 below).

I might invite him to reaffirm his faith using this
form from the baptism service:

Do you believe in God the Father, who made the world? — I believe and trust in him.

Do you believe and trust in his Son Jesus Christ, who redeemed mankind? — I believe and trust in him.

Do you believe and trust in his Holy Spirit, who gives life to the people of God? — I believe and trust in him.

3. I invite him to tell me if he has ever been involved in spiritualism, the occult, Satanism, or similar practices. The reason for this is that, if he has been dabbling in them, prayer for baptism in the Spirit can sometimes cause distressing reactions unless he is delivered from these influences first. If he admits to any serious involvement, then I postpone everything until he has been ministered to for deliverance. In such cases it is wise to seek the advice of someone who is experienced in this form of ministry.

4. I ask him if he is truly sorry for his sins and if he has asked God to forgive him through the cross and resurrection of Jesus Christ. He may want to mention things that are on his conscience. I make sure that he wants to turn his back on them (which is another way of saying he wants to repent).

As an Anglican priest, I might pronounce a formal absolution. If I was a layman, and if he admits to any serious sin, I might suggest he makes his confession to an ordained minister. But Christian practices vary considerably over this. There is nothing to prevent any Christian confessing his sins to another, provided the other is discreet and spiritually mature. However, many prefer to make their confession to an ordained minister, and this preference should always be respected.

Again, the baptismal form of renouncing evil and

turning to Jesus can be useful:

> *Do you turn to Christ? — I turn to Christ.*

> *Do you repent of your sins? — I repent of my sins.*

> *Do you renounce evil? — I renounce evil.*

5. I invite him to say a short prayer asking the Lord to send his Holy Spirit upon him. It helps individuals to vocalise their desires. It is an act of personal faith, particularly for someone who is not used to praying aloud, and it expresses the truth that the only Baptiser in the Spirit is Jesus (John 1.33) and that the only means of receiving the Spirit is through faith (Galatians 3.2).

6. I lay hands on his head and concentrate my attention on what the Holy Spirit might lead me to say. Usually my prayer begins by being addressed to God the Father, asking him to send his Spirit through Jesus Christ. Then I address God the Son, asking him to baptise the individual in the Spirit. Finally I address God the Holy Spirit, asking him to bring the gifts which he knows that individual requires to glorify God and to serve him. I do this slowly, though not taking more than a few minutes.

7. What happens next depends on the individual's response. Some sit quietly for several minutes, their eyes closed with a peaceful expression on their faces. Some breath deeply and shake, then suddenly burst out into cries of praise and thanksgiving (a Jamaican I knew was so excited that the legs of the chair on which he was sitting broke beneath him!) Some begin to speak in tongues. Some go into a kind of trance, to recover from it soon afterwards saying they were conscious

of the overshadowing presence of God. Some make no response at all.

8. If he speaks in tongues at this point, I join in quietly with him. I have occasionally been given a gift of interpretation at that moment. When I tell him what it is, he sometimes finds it amazingly relevant — and is gratified that it is a response to his own spiritual gift.

9. Then I invite him to join me in a prayer of thanksgiving to God for his wonderful gift. At this point a verse of scripture might come into my mind, in which case I share it with him.

10. Finally, I encourage him to find other Christians in his church or neighbourhood with whom he can pray regularly. The pastoral follow-up for those who have experienced baptism in the Spirit is very important.

I should point out, however, this programme is not always necessary. Sometimes the Lord brushes it aside and comes to individuals unexpectedly. And in large congregations or rallies, when many people come forward together to be baptised in the Spirit, I have to pray for them in a group. But unless there is guidance to the contrary, I aim to keep to the programme I have outlined.

10. How do I know if I have been baptised in the Spirit?

We know if we have been baptised in water, for either we remember the event ourselves or others tell us about it. We also have our baptism certificate as evidence.

Baptism in the Holy Spirit is different. We may remember a day when we received prayer with the laying on of hands for personal renewal, and we

may have had a memorable experience with a gift of
speaking in tongues. But years later, when that
memory fades and when the spiritual battle has
been hard, we may doubt the reality of what we
experienced.

It needs to be said again and again that baptism
in the Holy Spirit is not a status or a reward. It is a
relationship which the disciples of Jesus Christ are
privileged to have with God. And, like all relationships, it can grow stronger or weaker according
to how we respond to him.

When we ask Jesus to baptise us in the Holy
Spirit, he meets us where we are and invites us to
follow him with more reliance in his strength. We
receive his Spirit through faith: 'Having believed,
you were marked in him with a seal, the promised
Holy Spirit, who is a deposit guaranteeing our
inheritance until the redemption of those who are
God's possession — to the praise of his glory'
(Ephesians 1.13-14). The image of a seal is significant. A seal will mark a substance like wax into a
special shape but without altering the substance
itself. Wax remains wax but in the shape of the seal.

Similarly, the Spirit begins to shape us into the
kind of women and men God wants us to be,
without taking away from us all that belongs to our
human freedom — freedom of choice, for example,
with all that means in terms of temptation and
discipline. And the seal of the Spirit is like the
down-payment which promises the full sum of
money later. It is a sign that we are God's
merchandise — his possession. Looking back, we
should be able to see where we have come from in
our Christian pilgrimage, even if we feel we have
not come very far.

The answer to the question, then, is a matter of

spiritual discernment. Are we living the life of faith? Are we conscious that God's hand has been upon us? Is our relationship with others being changed? Does our attitude to them and to the circumstances in which we live reflect the belief that the Lord is sovereign? Do we experience an inner peace — not necessarily all the time, but as a basic disposition to which we return after moments of depression or anxiety? Does Christian devotion — prayer, worship, reflection on the scriptures — delight us even if we feel we are not very good at it? Do we find in ourselves an increasing detestation of sin and evil? Are there occasions when we are used by the Lord in unexpected ways?

I do not ask these questions expecting you to add up the number of affirmative answers as an indication of whether or not you are baptised in the Spirit! Rather, they are offered as pointers to help our discernment. And even if at times we feel that none of these things are happening to us, that does not necessarily mean that God's hand is not on us. Our feelings are unreliable guides where our spiritual condition is concerned. Paul could be exasperated with himself when he still found he was a prisoner to 'the law of sin' at work within him: 'What a wretched man I am! Who will rescue me from this body of death?' But then he went on in faith to claim for himself the victory which God had won for him over sin: 'Thanks be to God — through Jesus Christ our Lord!' (Romans 7.24-25).

Other Christians are in a better position to discern whether or not we are growing in the Spirit. One of the blessings of a Christian community (that is, any group of believers who meet frequently enough to know one another well) is to see how another person will gradually mature spiritually. It is not an exaggeration to say that, in those who have been baptised in the Spirit, a transfiguration will gently and slowly take place so that, over a number of years, they almost become different people from what they were before.

They themselves may not be conscious of this. Indeed, they will probably be more aware of their failings. But those who know them well will see the difference in a greater love of the Lord and of others, and a growing in God's wisdom which is not the same as the wisdom of riper years.

11. Is baptism in the Spirit the same as confirmation?

Before I can begin to answer this question, I must sketch briefly the story of how infant baptism and confirmation evolved.

In New Testament times the Greek *baptisma* was used to refer to a ritual washing, such as John's baptism for the remission of sins. At the baptism of Jesus, the Holy Spirit descended on the Messiah as he was coming up out of the river Jordan, showing that this ritual washing was more than a sign of the remission of sins; it was also a new encounter with God by his Spirit preparing people for judgement (Mark 1.10 and parallels).

After Pentecost, the apostolic church saw in the baptism at the river Jordan a revelation of what Christian baptism was meant to be. Through the death and resurrection of Jesus Christ, those who responded to the Gospel were initiated into a new life in him by the Holy Spirit. Baptism in water, therefore, was administered to those who repented of their sins, who believed in Christ, and who were open to the coming of the Spirit (Acts 2.38). When they were baptised, converts were taught to receive the Spirit by faith and to yield themselves to him. Then he would manifest himself in them through lives transformed by holiness and power. They would become a new creation (2 Corinthians 3.3), born of God (John 1.13), saved 'through the washing of rebirth and renewal by the Holy Spirit' (Titus 3.5). It is not known if children were baptised with their parents in New Testament times, but from the second century onwards there is increasing evidence that they were.

However, once the age of persecution passed, larger numbers of people sought the benefits of church membership, bringing their families with them. Baptism tended to become for many just a cultic or even a superstitious observance, with little real faith in Jesus Christ as Saviour, Lord, and Baptiser in the Spirit. It became the normal practice to bring infants to the font a day or two after their birth. As infant mortality was common, there was a strong desire to 'make them Christians' immediately in case they died (coupled with fears about what might happen to their souls if they died unbaptised). So the association of baptism with personal repentance, faith, and openness to the Spirit was weakened. Christian initiation became institutionalised.

Throughout early Christian history the administration of baptism was nearly always accompanied by the additional signs of laying on of hands and/or anointing. The baptism in the water of the font was usually performed by the priests or the deacons; the bishop presided over the service and did the anointing and the laying on of hands.

As the number of candidates (including infants) increased, it was not possible for bishops to preside

over every service of Christian initiation in their
area or diocese. The administration of the sacramental signs was therefore adapted to changing
circumstances. In the Orthodox East the local
priest baptised the baby and anointed the child
with oil which had been blessed by a bishop. In the
Catholic West the local priest also baptised the
baby, but the laying on of hands and anointing was
postponed until a bishop came into the locality —
often years later.

So it was that the bishop's role in the rites of
initiation came to be known as 'confirmation'
('strengthening' in the Spirit). Only privileged
families managed to arrange for a bishop to
administer both baptism and confirmation to their
children. Queen Elizabeth I was baptised and
confirmed when she was only a few days' old.

Those churches of the Reformation which
retained infant baptism and confirmation — administered by bishops among those who, like the
Anglicans and Lutherans, have retained episcopacy
— laid down that the candidates should reaffirm
the vows which had been made on their behalf
when they were christened. These candidates were
(and still are) encouraged to expect a strengthening
of the Spirit through prayer and the laying on of
hands, to equip them for a life of Christian witness.
In recent years, since the Second Vatican Council,
Roman Catholic practices have developed along the
same lines.

How, then, does baptism in the Spirit relate to
this? Since confirmation is a sign that when we are
baptised we are not only regenerated by the Holy
Spirit but also strengthened and equipped by him
for our Christian discipleship, there can be a very
close connection between confirmation and Spirit

baptism. Indeed, some bishops and priests prepare
candidates to be open to fresh gifts of the Spirit
through their confirmation. Stories are told of
candidates being given the gift of tongues when the
bishop lays his hands on them with prayer, or
shortly afterwards.

But, of course, there is nothing automatic about
this. Baptism in the Spirit is the beginning of a new
encounter with the living God, when we learn to
accept that we are not only redeemed by Jesus
Christ but also immersed by him in the Spirit. This
spiritual encounter cannot be invoked by rituals. It
is an act of God's sovereign will, at a time and place
chosen by him. All the church can do is to
encourage those who are being prepared for confirmation to be ready to be baptised in the Spirit —
and to go on being immersed in the Spirit for the
rest of their lives. This is what a prayer (based on
Isaiah 11.2) used at confirmations requests:

> *Almighty and everlasting God,*
> *you have given your servants new birth*
> *in baptism by water and the Spirit,*
> *and have forgiven them all their sins.*
> *Let your Holy Spirit rest upon them:*
> *the Spirit of wisdom and understanding;*
> *the Spirit of counsel and inward strength;*
> *the Spirit of knowledge and true godliness;*
> *and let their delight be in the fear of the Lord.*

One final point. What I have said above does not
mean that the Holy Spirit is absent from infant
baptism and later confirmation. In the case of an
infant baptism, God answers the prayers which his
people offer in Jesus Christ's name through the use
of water as a sacramental sign.

Problems arise when we try to define precisely
what the Spirit does at such a moment. Obviously

the infant is not 'saved' in the sense of having repented and embraced Jesus Christ in an act of personal faith. But Orthodox, Catholic and some Reformed churches teach that God brings that infant within the company of his people who are being saved and that, in that environment, the child has every opportunity of growing into faith himself or herself. Confirmation is then extremely meaning-ful when it is associated with such a step of faith, when the candidate openly confesses Jesus as his or her Saviour and Lord.

12. What is the connection between conversion and baptism in the Spirit?

The act of personal conversion is a work of the Holy Spirit in us. It is only by his power that we can come to the point were we want to turn to Jesus Christ as our Lord and Saviour. We do not become believers through our own natural efforts. God has to energise us in order to overcome the effects of our sinful nature which separate us from him.

This is not to say that we don't have a choice. We do choose whether or not to turn to him; but we are made aware of that choice by him and, in the act of choosing, he meets us by his Spirit to illuminate and strengthen us.

When Peter confessed that Jesus was the Christ, the Son of the living God, the Lord said to him, 'Blessed are you, Simon son of Jonah, for this was not revealed to you by man, but by my Father in heaven' (Matthew 16.17). The apostolic letters teach that the way in which the Father reveals the Son is through his Holy Spirit. 'This is how you can recognise the Spirit of God: Every spirit that acknowledges that Jesus Christ has come in the flesh is from God, but every spirit that does not acknowledge Jesus is not from God' (1 John 4.2-3). And Paul wrote, 'I tell you that no one who is speaking by the Spirit of God... can say, "Jesus is Lord," except by the Holy Spirit' (1 Corinthians 12.3).

Yet there is a distinction between the work of the Spirit in bringing the believer to new birth (regeneration) and being baptised in the Spirit. Conversion is a once-for-all, unrepeatable event. In the New Testament it is described as a turning from the darkness of idolatry, sin and the rule of Satan, to the worship and the service of the true God. It is an exercise of repentance and faith, which Jesus Christ and Paul link together as summing up the moral demand of the Gospel (Mark 1.15; Acts 20.21). Repentance means a change of mind and heart towards God; faith means belief in his word and trust in his Christ; conversion covers both. So the one who is converted and baptised in water can be described as being 'born of water and the Spirit' (John 3.5).

For his Christian discipleship, however, the believer needs the continuous and growing presence of the Spirit in his life, and it is initiation into this relationship which is described as 'being baptised in the Holy Spirit'. It is a gift of the Spirit which looks beyond regeneration to the future life of the believer in the community of God's people as, in the name of Jesus, he serves the kingdom of God. The risen Christ promised his disciples before his ascension; 'You will receive power when the Holy Spirit comes on you; and you will be my witnesses in Jerusalem, and in all Judaea and Samaria, and to the ends of the earth' (Acts 1.8). That is the purpose of Spirit-baptism.

Ideally, conversion should include that, too. And, if the enquirer has been instructed in the Gospel thoroughly, we could expect him to be baptised in the Spirit about the same time as he makes a public confession of faith and receives water baptism.

I was once present in a Baptist church when a young woman was brought for baptism. Before a large congregation she made a brief testimony, describing how she had renounced her former way of life and come to faith in Jesus Christ. She then descended into the water to be baptised by the minister while the congregation quietly sang choruses. When she came out of the water, she knelt as the minister and one or two deacons laid their hands and prayed for the gift of the Holy Spirit.

Immediately she began praising God in a new language, leaping up and holding her hands in the air in great joy. Almost at once the whole congregation stood and began singing in the Spirit. As the singing died away, someone was inspired to utter an interpretation, in which God reassured his newly born-again child that he would be with her to guide her through what she had to face as a consequence of her conversion and confession of faith.

It was a moving moment. I doubt whether there was a dry eye in the church! If there is such a thing as a 'model conversion' this was the nearest to it that I have ever experienced — and baptism in the Spirit was all part of the package!

But in most cases the act of repenting and turning in faith to Christ is such an overwhelming experience that it is not until later the convert comes to realise the significance of baptism in the Spirit and seeks it for himself. When that happens, it seems like a 'second blessing' to him; but theologically it is a continuation of the Spirit's work, begun before his conversion and now equipping him for his Christian witness in the world.

13. Can children be baptised in the Spirit?

Many families involved in the charismatic renewal relate how their children have experienced baptism in the Spirit and speaking in tongues. Instances have been known of this happening to children as young as seven or eight.

This need not surprise us. Children have an open and trusting attitude towards the Lord, and in their early years they follow their parents' lead in ideas, expectations and prayer. Children should not be pushed into receiving prayer for baptism in the Spirit. But if they ask sincerely and persistently, then they should be taught simply what it means to be filled with the Spirit and prayed for with the laying on of hands in the same way as for an adult.

Children usually receive the gift of tongues very easily. Perhaps this is because they are less inhibited than adults. Perhaps it is because they are skilful imitators! The fact that initially a gift of tongues may be imitated is not to be discouraged. Many adults begin to pray in tongues when they have heard others doing the same, and some degree of imitation is almost inevitable at first. The test for the authenticity of this gift is the same as for any other charism: does it in the long run help us to glorify the Lord and to serve others in his name?

As in other religious practices, however, children require guidance and encouragement. They also need to be integrated into regular and appropriate acts of corporate prayer, either with members of the family, or with church services, or with a prayer group which is able to accommodate them for at least part of its meeting. If your child is led into these and similar experiences, trust the Lord to guide him as you seek to be obedient together.

But don't be discouraged if a few years' later he seems to drop his prayer and worship. We all need to be renewed in the Spirit daily, and there are some days when we fail to accept the renewing grace of God into our lives, as we well know! Children and young people are no different. In the growing and exciting years of teenage other things — especially their peer group — can become the focus of their attention.

Yet their early experience of the Holy Spirit's working in their lives will not be forgotten. Go on loving them, and so being a channel of God's love; and one day they will hear again the Lord's call to follow him — and they will obey.

14. Why do many clergy refuse to re-baptise those who have been renewed in the Holy Spirit and request this?

This problem occurs in those churches (notably Anglican and Roman Catholic) which teach that baptism is a sacrament which can only be administered once to an individual. When an individual has experienced baptism in the Spirit, he often feels this is his first real encounter with the Lord and he wants to respond by offering himself for water baptism — usually by immersion.

The request puts the priest in a difficult position. If that member has already been baptised (and confirmed), the priest is not allowed by his church to re-baptise him. To understand why the church lays this down, we have to answer the key question:

What happens when an individual is baptised in water in the name of the Father and of the Son and of the Holy Spirit (Matthew 28.19)?

The teaching of the New Testament is that baptism signifies what God has done for our salvation through the mediating work of Christ. Baptism is a dying to self and a being reborn to a new life in Christ. When we are baptised, we are made a new creation (2 Corinthians 5.17). '(God) saved us through the washing of regeneration and renewal by the Holy Spirit, which he poured out on us generously through Jesus Christ our Saviour, so that, having been justified by his grace, we might become heirs having the hope of eternal life' (Titus 3.5-6). The practice of taking a new name (a 'Christian name') reflects this truth: our proper name is not our surname, which is generic, but our Christian name, which is our own.

Even though we still have to die physically, death has no power over us. We are already risen with Christ (Colossians 2.12,3.1). We share his heavenly reign. The Holy Spirit is given to us as an 'earnest', a foretaste, of what is to come, and he unites us with other members of the body of Christ, the church.

But, we might ask — and this is the next key question — does this mean then, everyone is regenerate (reborn) when they receive baptism, no matter what they believe (or don't believe) at the time? And are they still regenerate when, like babies, they are not conscious of what is happening to them?

Throughout the centuries most Christians have held that the New Testament reveals that in baptism God always responds with his forgiveness and grace when we celebrate the sacrament with the intention of obeying his commission. In other

words, what matters when we are baptised is what
God does for us, not what we feel or believe (or
don't feel or don't believe). Baptism is an act of
divine grace in response to the prayer of the church,
not a reward for our conversion.

If we didn't believe this, then we should never
know whether or not a particular individual has
been baptised. There would always be the nagging
question, 'Suppose I didn't have enough repentance or faith when I was baptised? Have I really
been made a child of God?'

So the church teaches that sacraments are
covenanted and objective means of receiving God's
grace which do not ultimately depend on how the
recipient is feeling at the time they are administered. To be effective, of course, that recipient must
make a personal response to God in faith — if not at
the moment of receiving the sacrament then later
(perhaps years later, in the case of an infant's
baptism). Nevertheless, on God's side sacraments
always offer his grace.

As *Article XXV* of the Church of England puts it:

> *Sacraments ordained of Christ be not only badges or tokens of
> Christian men's profession, but rather they be certain sure
> witnessed, and effectual signs of grace, and God's good will
> towards us, by the which he doth work invisibly in us, and doth
> not only quicken, but also strengthen our faith in him.*

Therefore if an individual has once been baptised
— no matter whether or not he knew about it —
God has fulfilled his part in the celebration of that
sacrament. To repeat the sacramental sign — for
whatever purpose — is to proclaim publicly that we
do not believe God keeps his word.

And that, very briefly, is why many clergy are not
allowed to re-baptise. Theologically it isn't possible

to baptise anyone again — any more than it is possible for an individual to be physically re-born once he has come from the mother's womb.

Charismatics who seek re-baptism can be encouraged to make their confession to a priest and/or to make a fresh affirmation of their faith before the congregation on an appropriate occasion. Services for renewing baptismal promises are provided in many service books for such occasions.

I ought to point out, however, that this understanding of what God does when someone is baptised is not accepted by all Christians. Since the Reformation the practice of 'believers' baptism' has spread among certain traditions — Baptists, Pentecostals, and many independent Evangelical Churches. They hold that the sacrament should not be administered to an individual who has not made a conscious choice about the matter, and they argue that, since babies were not baptised in New Testament times, they should not be baptised now.

Consequently some of the ministers of these churches are willing to 're-baptise' a person who was baptised in infancy.

THE GIFTS OF THE SPIRIT

15. What are spiritual gifts?

The New Testament reveals that what Jesus said and did was the result of his close union in the Holy Spirit with his heavenly Father. The Spirit was active in his incarnate life from the moment of his conception in the womb of the virgin Mary to his resurrection from the grave (Luke 1.35; Romans 8.11). At his baptism the Spirit came upon him to equip him for his public ministry (Matthew 3.13-17; Mark 1.9-13; Luke 3.21-22; John 1.32-34), so that his preaching and his miracles were manifestations of divine power.

The same Spirit came upon the disciples of Christ at Pentecost, also equipping them for all that they said and did in Jesus' name (Acts 2.1- 4); and the Spirit comes upon present-day disciples as they speak and act in Jesus' name. It is these acts of the Holy Spirit in and through Christians which are called 'spiritual gifts' — gifts of the Spirit's power to enable us to act as Jesus' disciples. They are available in any situation in which we may find ourselves — in the family, among our friends and acquaintances, in the church (both in worship services and in other things), in society, and so on.

We find the most detailed teaching in the New Testament about spiritual gifts in 1 Corinthians 12-14. There Paul points out that spiritual gifts are only exercised when they are an expression of a life-union with Jesus Christ: 'No-one can say, "Jesus is Lord," except by the Holy Spirit' (1 Corinthians 12.3). Anything which does not exult the lordship of Christ, no matter how spectacular, does not qualify as a spiritual gift.

In 12.4-6 spiritual gifts are described in three ways: as *charismata* (gifts), as *diakonia* (ministries), and as *energemata* (workings). By employing these three words the apostle was expressing something about (1) the origin of the gifts, (2) the manner in which they are experienced in the church, and (3) their purpose.

(1) The word *charismata* indicates the origin of the spiritual gifts — from the grace *(charis)* of God which takes concrete form in words and actions. The literal meaning of *charisma* is 'a present'. Ephesians 4.8 tells us that the ascended Christ gave presents to his body, the church: 'When he ascended on high, he led captives in his train and gave gifts to men.'

(2) The word *diakonia*, ministries or services, shows how spiritual gifts are experienced. It is as others minister to us, or serve us, in Jesus' name that we encounter spiritual gifts. That ministry or service reflects the work of Christ himself: 'The Son of Man did not come to be served, but to serve, and to give his life as a ransom for many' (Matthew 20.28). A ministry is not a matter of lowliness or humiliation, but of willing and loving action.

(3) The word *energemata*, workings or energies, demonstrates that spiritual gifts have observable effects. We should expect things to happen. When a Christian exercises a spiritual gift, he is acting as a member of the body of Christ; that is to say, Christ himself is working through that person. And the result gives glory to God. 'Gifts' or 'presents' is not an entirely satisfactory translation because in English these words imply that what is given becomes the property of the one who receives it. Spiritual gifts, on the other hand, in no sense belong to the Christian who exercises them. What is given is God's grace by his Spirit. Spiritual gifts are withdrawn when the one who exercises them is

disobedient to God.

'There are different kinds of gifts, but the same Spirit' (12.4). In the Bibliothéque Nationale in Paris there is a ninth-century illuminated manuscript, called the Sacramentary of Archbishop Drogo, which contains a small picture of the disciples in the upper room on the day of Pentecost. They are looking up to heaven where the ascended Christ is directing a dove out of whose beak streams a flame of fire. As the flame descends, it divides into separate tongues, and each tongue rests on the head of a disciple.

The picture highlights in a primitive manner the profound scriptural truth. Spiritual gifts are many and various, but they are distributed by the one Spirit and, if they are used as the Spirit wills, they possess an inherent unity which embraces their diversities. They have a single purpose in working for the common good of the Christian community (12.7).

Certain consequences stem from this:

1. When the exercise of spiritual gifts causes division in the church, we must discern carefully the reason for that division. Is it caused because sin is being exposed as the Holy Spirit convicts individuals and groups of their disobediences? Or is it caused because there is a lack of love among those who exercise ministries in the church? If it is the second reason, then we must doubt whether those ministries are truly of the Spirit.

2. Ultimately the exercise of spiritual gifts will point both those who minister and those who receive ministry to Christ. Jesus said of the Spirit, 'He will bring glory to me by taking from me what is mine and making it known to you' (John 16.14).

3. Gifts of the Spirit will be recognised because

they result in greater love. The passages in the New Testament which teach about spiritual gifts (Romans 12.3-8; 1 Corinthians 12-14; Ephesians 4.7-16; 1 Peter 4.8-11) all relate the exercise of spiritual gifts to manifestations of God's love within the Christian community.

16. How many spiritual gifts are there?

The New Testament mentions over twenty-five, but the lists in the apostolic letters are not intended to be exhaustive. The 'manifold grace of God' can be experienced in many different ways. There is, for example, no reference to the composition of music for worship, the writing of hymns, songs, poems and books, or other artistic achievements which glorify God, though the Old Testament recognised the power of God in the craftsmen who beautified the temple (Exodus 31.1-11, 35.30-35).

In the early Pentecostal churches, the charisms listed in the New Testament were regarded as having a special scriptural authority which set them over and above any other manifestations. The question was asked, 'Where in your congregation are the apostles, prophets, evangelists, pastors and teachers?'

Within the charismatic renewal, however, a broader view of spiritual gifts is normal. What God equips his people with today may not always be exactly identifiable with a New Testament charism. By the very nature of things, the apostles could not foresee that one day special gifts would be required for presenting the gospel on the radio and television!

When we compare the New Testament lists we see that names overlap, or that the same spiritual

gift is mentioned by a different name; elsewhere
the charism is referred to as something being done
by somebody:

Rom 12.6-8	1 Cor 12.4-11	1 Cor 12.28-32	Eph 4.11	1 Pet 4.10-11
		apostles	apostles	
prophesying	prophecy	prophets	prophets	
			evangelists	
			pastors	
teaching		teachers	teachers	speaks
encouraging				
	faith			
	miraculous	work		
	powers	miracles		
gifts of	gifts of	gifts of		
healing	healing	healing		
serves		able to		serves
		help		
contributing				
show mercy				
leadership		administration		
	wisdom			
	knowledge			
	discerning			
	of spirits			
	tongues	tongues		
	interpretation	interpretation		

There are references to spiritual gifts in
1 Corinthians 13.1-3: tongues, prophecy, understanding all mysteries and all knowledge, faith, giving
away all possessions, surrendering one's body to the
flames (or giving oneself up to the most painful of
deaths for some great cause). In 1 Corinthians
14.26 there are directions about how various

spiritual gifts are to be used in worship — a hymn, or a word of instruction, a revelation, a tongue and an interpretation — as well as a discussion about the use of tongues, interpretations and prophecies generally.

Spiritual gifts are defined as 'functions in the body of Christ' (Romans 12.4), 'manifestations of the Spirit for the common good' (1 Corinthians 12.7), 'works of service, so that the body of Christ may be built up until we all reach unity in the faith and in the knowledge of the Son of God and become mature, attaining to the whole measure of the fulness of Christ' (Ephesians 4.12-13), and given 'to serve others, administering God's grace in its various forms' (1 Peter 4.10).

In books about the Holy Spirit, spiritual gifts are sometimes referred to as 'charisms'. This term was popularised by Roman Catholic charismatics and scholars after the Second Vatican Council, the documents of which strongly supported the biblical understanding of spiritual gifts. One important passage is in the Council's *Constitution on the Church* (Chapter 12). After teaching about the sacramental nature of the church and its prophetic ministry, the *Constitution* says (in the slightly quaint language of the official English translation):

> It is not only through the sacraments and church ministries that the Holy Spirit sanctifies and leads the people of God and enriches it with virtues. Allotting his gifts 'to everyone according as he will' (1 Corinthians 12.11), he distributes special graces among the faithful of every rank. By these gifts he makes them fit and ready to undertake the various tasks and offices advantageous for the renewal and upbuilding of the church, according to the words of the apostle, 'The manifestation of the Spirit is given to

everyone for the profit' (1 Corinthians 12.7). These charismatic gifts, whether they be the most outstanding or the more simple and widely diffused, are to be received with thanksgiving and consolation for they are exceedingly suitable and useful for the needs of the church.

Still, extraordinary gifts are not to be rashly sought after nor are the fruits of apostolic labour to be presumptuously expected from them. In any case, judgement as to their genuineness and proper use belongs to those who preside over the church, and to whose special competence it belongs not indeed to extinguish the Spirit, but to test all things and hold fast to that which is good (cf. 1 Thessalonians 5. 19-21).

It follows, then, that any act, either by an individual, a group or a church which manifests the grace of God in glorifying Jesus Christ and in promoting Christian unity and maturity is a spiritual gift.

It is notable that each of the passages listed above is set in the context of the love of God, so anything which does not in some measure reveal that love is not an authentic charism.

It is also notable that the New Testament teaches that manifestations have to be tested — discerned (a vital spiritual gift) — a point echoed in the *Constitution* quoted above. This will be discussed in answer to the relevant question.

17. Does everyone have spiritual gifts?

The straightforward answer to this is, Yes. Everyone who turns to Jesus Christ receives the Holy Spirit, and with the Spirit comes the spiritual gifts for that person to serve the Lord in his or her life.

A more detailed answer begins with the words,

'Well, it all depends....'

For one thing, it depends on what sort of spiritual gifts we are thinking of. If I, as a Christian, am content with saying my prayers and going to church, but doing little else as a disciple of Christ, then it is unlikely I will exercise any of the charisms listed in the New Testament. I will be doing very little 'for the common good' (1 Corinthians 12.7). I will hardly be contributing to the building up of the body of Christ (Ephesians 4.12). I will be like the servant in the parable who received one talent and hid it in the ground until his master returned (Matthew 25.25). If I never take any initiative as a Christian or make a stand for what I believe is true and just; if I do nothing for the Christian community in teaching, in evangelising, in the encouragement of others, or in hospitality, administration or any other form of service, it is difficult to see how I can exercise any spiritual gifts.

For another thing, it depends on how far I trust in the Holy Spirit to equip me for what I undertake in the Lord's name. If I play an organ or a guitar for worship, do I regard it as a skill the Spirit has given me for the service of God's people, or do I regard it as an opportunity to demonstrate before an audience my ability as a musician? Or, to take another example, if I learn that certain individuals at work or in the neighbourhood are being treated unjustly, do I just grumble about it at home, or do I endeavour to take some initiative to put the injustice right, after praying about what I could do and seeking advice and support?

My attitude and my response will determine whether or not I experience the power and guidance of the Spirit. And, if he equips me with charisms for the task, I may have to face opposition,

misunderstanding and even hardship. Being a
disciple of the Crucified does not usually come easy!

As I said in a previous answer, the expression
'having spiritual gifts' is unsatisfactory. 1 Peter 4.10
speaks of 'receiving spiritual gifts', and that is a
better way of putting it. We do not 'possess'
charisms; they do not belong to us. They are powers
of God exercised in and through us when we submit
ourselves obediently to him. They are only 'gifts' in
the sense that the Spirit is 'giving himself' to us in
response to our Christian obedience.

This qualification helps us to discern how spiritual gifts are to be used. If we remember that
charisms are not ours but God's, then we have no
cause to be jealous because another person has a
more spectacular or successful ministry than we
have. He is receiving what God is giving him; we
are to receive what God gives us.

All ministries are important to the Lord, no
matter how spectacular or hidden they may be.
That is what Paul emphasised when he compared
members of the church with different members of a
human body. They require one another if the body
is to function properly: 'The body is a unity, though
it is made up of many parts; and though all its parts
are many, they form one body... The eye cannot say
to the hand, "I don't need you!" And the head
cannot say to the feet, "I don't need you!"' (1
Corinthians 12.12,21).

What members of a congregation can do is to
help one another realise the spiritual gifts which
God has given them and encourage each other in
exercising those charisms as the Lord wills. There
are many, many Christians through whom he
wants to do this but who fail to recognise what he
can do through them if they let him.

We may not always be given the charisms we think we would like to have; but if we and the rest of the congregation can forget self and seek God's guidance in what he wants us to do in Jesus' name, we shall discover that everyone does indeed 'have' spiritual gifts.

18. Is a natural talent the same as a spiritual gift?

Two basic Christian truths lie behind the answer to this question. One is that 'God saw all that he made, and it was very good' (Genesis 1.31). The other is that what God has created has been contaminated by sin. We are a 'fallen' creation. Natural gifts — and by these I mean the different abilities and skills which people have — can reflect the goodness of God as our Creator; but they can also reflect the sinfulness of our fallen world.

In fact, almost any natural ability has both a light and a dark side to it. Take any example we can think of — in academic, artistic, athletic, educational, engineering, literary, medical, musical, scientific skills, and so on — and we can soon think of ways in which any one of them can be used for good or evil purposes.

But where a natural talent is used for good, then it manifests the goodness of God who created it. No one else can produce goodness. The world came into being through the power of God's Spirit, and where the world reflects God's goodness, then there the Spirit is at work gifting women and men through that goodness. Bezalel was filled with the Spirit of God 'to engage in all kinds of craftsmanship' for making the furnishings of the Tent of Meeting (Exodus 31.1-11). And we can discern the working of God in many areas of life where individuals and groups promote the wellbeing of people in accordance with the will of God.

Such natural talents can be called 'gifts of the Spirit' in a general sense; they come from our Creator and they are signs of his power. But in the New Testament the term *charismata* is reserved for those abilities and skills which are dedicated to his service for the building up of the church. So if we are to be faithful to New Testament terminology, it is only when a natural talent is used for these purposes that it can properly be called a gift of the Spirit.

Though some Christians exercise their charisms effectively without any training, most are better ministering in the Spirit after they have been given instruction and practised their ministry under the guidance of a more experienced leader. Gifts of teaching, prophecy, administration, leadership, together with many others, are of greater value if those who manifest them are willing to learn.

A subsidiary question is sometimes asked, Are all authentic charisms miraculous? The early Pente-costals stressed the miraculous element of the spiritual gifts listed in the New Testament, particu-larly prophecies, tongues, interpretations, healings, and they taught that it is only when this miraculous element is present that manifestations can truly be called gifts of the Spirit.

Within the charismatic movement, however, this definition has not been accepted. While it is true there are miraculous elements in our experience of some of these charisms — sudden healings, for example, or prophecies which have been remark-ably vindicated — many spiritual gifts are simply natural abilities which are blessed by God in such a

way that they point us to Jesus as well as to those
who exercise them.

Take teaching, for example. A man can be 'a
born teacher' because he has a natural ability to
communicate knowledge and to inspire enthusiasm
in those who learn from him. And, because he is
God's creature, we can say that his teaching
abilities are a gift from God, even if the teacher does
not have any personal commitment to the Lord.
However, the result of his teaching may be very
different if he is a disciple of Jesus. The Holy Spirit
will take his natural ability to teach and transfigure
it into a spiritual gift, so that those who learn from
him might sense the presence of Christ in what he
teaches and in the way he teaches it.

This leads to a further practical question: If we
want something done, should we go to a Christian
craftsman rather than a non-Christian one, even if
the former is in fact less able than the latter in that
particular craft? For example, is it lack of faith on
our part if we choose a good non-Christian dentist
rather than a less skilful Christian one?

Ralph Vaughan Williams edited two hymn
books, wrote magnificent tunes to new hymns
'Down Ampney' for 'Come down, O Love Divine',
and composed music for dramatic presentations of
Job (a ballet) and *Pilgrim's Progress* (an opera). Yet
he remained an agnostic all his life!

When we consider the question of relative skills,
therefore, we must try to foresee the consequences
of our choice. Will it give greater glory to God to
have the task done well by an agnostic, or to have it
done less well by someone who is a believer?

19. How can we be sure that a spiritual gift is genuine?

A friend of mine, who has been much involved in the charismatic renewal for many years, was asked this question. He paused before he answered, and then said this: 'I reckon about two-thirds of what passes for spiritual gifts are phoney.'

There was a shocked silence. 'Could it really be like that?' I could see his listeners saying to themselves.

Then he leaned forward. 'But think what that means,' he went on, excitement mounting in his voice. 'It means one-third are from God!'

There is a passage in Paul's earliest known letter which is full of inspired advice about this problem.

> Be joyful always; pray continually; give thanks in all circumstances, for this is God's will for you in Christ Jesus. Do not put out the Spirit's fire; do not treat prophecies with contempt. Test everything. Hold on to the good. Avoid every kind of evil. May God himself, the God of peace, sanctify you through and through. May your whole spirit, soul and body be kept blameless at the coming of our Lord Jesus Christ. The one who calls you is faithful and he will do it.
>
> (1 Thessalonians 5.16-24)

The picture given here is of a Christian community which is focused on the Lord and growing in loving unity with one another. Thanksgiving and joy are the keynotes in their prayers. That joy and thanksgiving springs from a deep faith in what God has done for his people in the past and in what he will do for them in the future. They are aware of Christ's continuing presence.

They do not attempt to quench the Spirit through erroneous teaching or through public arguments. They take all manifestations as authentic and treat them seriously. But they also test everything.

To see that this testing is done in an orderly manner is one of the most important responsibilities of the pastoral leadership of the congregation. When leaders are chosen, two of the qualities looked for are wisdom and discernment. Wisdom is insight into the will of God for individuals and groups, whoever they might be. Discernment is a special charism which enables leaders to pick out what is true and what is false in everything that is presented as a gift of the Spirit.

Spiritual gifts will not contradict anything that is revealed in the scriptures. Indeed, there will be a continuity with the ministry of Jesus Christ and of the apostolic church in what is manifested. The goodness of God will shine through these charisms so that we find ourselves experiencing in a mysterious way the presence and power of Christ himself. We, and those involved with us, will be built up through the spiritual gifts and will witness the signs of God's kingdom in the consequences which flow from them.

There will be nothing evil about any spiritual gift. Indeed, as a result of experiencing a spiritual gift, we shall want to avoid anything tainted with wickedness. Rather, we will want to grow in holiness. So the charism will be wholesome, healing, revealing and strengthening — and it will encourage us to live and proclaim the gospel all the more hopefully.

Those are the characteristics of spiritual gifts, and the setting within which they are exercised and controlled, which enables us to decide whether or not they are genuine.

20. What is the difference between the fruit of the Spirit and the gifts of the Spirit?

These descriptions are mixed up by those who have not studied their Bibles carefully!

The phrase 'the fruit of the Spirit' comes from that section of Paul's epistle to the Galatians where he is explaining the right way to use our Christian liberty (Galatians 5.13-26). Our freedom from bondage to the Law, says the apostle, must not become an excuse for selfishness. We should not abuse our liberty by permitting our old evil nature to have its way. Instead, we should practise liberty in love: 'serve one another in love'.

Our 'sinful nature' (which in Greek Paul called *sarx*, 'flesh') is the capacity to sin which exists in all of us, even when we are Christians. It is the enemy inside us that would destroy our freedom in Christ and bring us into worse bondage. Therefore, each child of God needs a helping and restraining hand to guard against his own sinful nature.

We find this help in the Paraclete or Advocate dwelling within us. By the Spirit we can have strength to keep in step with him day by day and not to surrender to the impulses and desires of the flesh. By the Spirit we can put to death and rise above the negative attitudes and evil deeds which are characteristic of our sinful nature (Romans 8.13). If we belong to Christ, we shall have made the decision to consider the flesh, with its passions and desires, as a crucified thing. This will mean a continuous battle, because the indwelling Spirit and the sinful nature are hostile to each other. (Paul develops this in Romans 7.14-25.)

After listing many of the sinful practices of the flesh, the apostle contrasts them with the results of the indwelling Spirit. He paints them as the luscious fruit of a marvellously fertile plant: 'The fruit of the Spirit is love, joy, peace, patience, kindness, goodness, faithfulness, gentleness and self-control.' In this he is very close to Christ's own teaching about himself as the vine and his disciples as the fruit-bearing branches (John 15.1-8).

Paul uses the term 'fruit' in the singular, underlining the unity and coherence for those who walk in the Spirit. The change from 'the acts of the sinful nature' to 'the fruit of the Spirit' shifts the emphasis away from the human endeavour to that of spiritual growth. The first three deal with inward qualities which mainly affect the self although of course they affect attitudes to others. The remaining six are more socially orientated.

Briefly, the implications of these fruit is as follows. *Love* is at the heart of the gospel (it is the subject of Paul's great hymn in 1 Corinthians 13). Christian love is vastly different from contemporary ideas about it, for it is patterned on the love of God for man as revealed in Jesus Christ. Both his love and ours are the produce of the same Spirit. *Joy* and *peace* are often mentioned in Paul's letters: they are the result of our hope in God.

Patience means being willing to bear up under the strains and stresses of life, knowing that in the end the Lord is our ruler. *Kindness* and *goodness* are passive and active sides of our relationships with others. *Gentleness* is not a weak virtue but a deliberate submission to God leading to harmony. *Faithfulness* is complete reliability in our discipleship. *Self-control* is mastery over our natural desires — or, rather, Spirit-control through our being willing to open ourselves to him.

The passage rounds off with the apostle's assertion that no law can produce the fruit of the Spirit. The fruit is so completely opposite to what the believer's sinful nature produces that he must be willing to crucify the latter in order that the former may grow.

The picture of the vine, then, is a vivid illustration of the maturing Christian life. The best fruit springs from soil which is fertile and cultivated and from branches which are pruned regularly. And the fruit will bear a marked resemblance to those same virtues which are perfectly exhibited in the life of our Lord, for they are the result of his life in us.

'By their fruit you will recognise them.' Jesus' warning in his teaching on the tree and its fruit (Matthew 7.15-25) makes a clear distinction between the gifts of the Spirit and the fruit of the Spirit. He told his disciples that prayer, prophecy, exorcisms and miraculous works are not in themselves proofs that those who are used in these charisms are filled with the Spirit. The Lord can work in his sovereign power even through those who do not acknowledge him.

The basic difference between the gifts of the Spirit and the fruit of the Spirit, then, is this. The gifts are signs of God's power which do not depend on the personal holiness of those who manifest these signs; the fruit are unmistakable signs of holiness in a person's life which spring from a growing unity with and obedience to Christ.

SPEAKING IN TONGUES, INTERPRETATIONS AND PROPHECIES

21. What is 'speaking in tongues'?

Speaking in tongues has attracted much attention because it seems such an irrational thing for a modern Christian to do.

The phrase 'speaking in tongues' was used in older translations of the New Testament to translate the Greek, *glossolalia*. This word is derived from (1) *glossa*, which means both 'tongue' as our physical organ of taste and speech, and also 'tongue' as the manner in which we speak, our language, and (2) *laleo*, meaning 'to speak'. Modern versions of the New Testament translate glossolalia as 'speaking in languages'. The NIV has 'tongues' in the text and 'languages' in the margin. Within the charismatic renewal it is commonly referred to as 'tongues'.

The only reference to it in the gospels is in Mark 16.17, where the risen Christ prophesies that those who believe the gospel will 'speak in new tongues.' In Acts glossolalia accompanies the descent of the Holy Spirit on the followers of Jesus on the day of Pentecost: 'All of them were filled with the Holy Spirit and began to speak in other tongues (marg. languages) as the Spirit enabled them' (Acts 2.4). Speaking in tongues also occurred when the Spirit was given to Cornelius and his household (Acts 10.46) and to the disciples at Ephesus (Acts 19.6).

'Speaking in different kinds of tongues' is one of the nine gifts of the Spirit listed by Paul in 1 Corinthians 12.7-11. In verse 30 he asked, 'Do all speak in tongues?' — and the Greek form of his question implies that he expected the answer, No. This is the reply to those who ask if baptism in the Spirit is always accompanied by speaking in tongues. The gift can be given when an individual

Christian is praying for baptism in the Spirit, or shortly afterwards; but it is not an essential sign of it. It is worth remembering that Paul also taught the gift of tongues is valueless unless it is exercised with love (13.1), and it will pass away at the second coming (13.8).

The apostle then explained how the charism is to be used in the Christian congregation. 'Anyone who speaks in a tongue does not speak to men' (who cannot understand what is said) 'but to God' (who inspires what is said and therefore understands it, even though it is unintelligible by normal human standards). Paul may have had in mind what he wrote in Romans 8.26: 'The Spirit helps us in our weaknesses. We do not know what we ought to pray for, but the Spirit himself intercedes for us with groans that words cannot express.'

Known languages are sometimes inadequate for expressing our deepest hopes and desires. At other times we do not know what words to use that are appropriate for a particular — especially a critical — situation. In these instances we offer our voice to God and let him use the sounds we make (trusting they are inspired by his Spirit) as our prayer to him.

It is often in such situations that individual Christians discover they have been given this charism. They are longing to pray more faithfully, or to be equipped by God's grace for some task they believe he is calling them to do. They speak out random syllables and consonants which initially seem like gobbledegook but then flow into a shape and rhythm that can be beautiful and impressive.

With some people the experience is so new and vibrant that they are emotionally affected — weeping, laughing, shaking, even falling to the floor. With others the experience is quiet and peaceful, leaving them with a fresh sense of God's indwelling presence. And with others there is no discernible emotion or inner sense — just a hope that a novel dimension of prayer has been opened up for them.

'He who prays in tongues edifies himself' (14.4): he 'builds himself up' or, rather, he allows God to continue that process of spiritual maturing which is essential to any Christian pilgrimage. Of course, tongues does not do this automatically; as with all spiritual gifts, it requires our obedient co-operation if it is to be fruitful in our lives. Nor is tongues the only form of devotion that builds us up. Paul is simply affirming that tongues can be a means of strengthening our commitment to Jesus Christ and our openness to the Holy Spirit as children of God.

In this chapter 14 of 1 Corinthians the apostle stresses the greater value of prophecy as a gift of the Spirit in a congregation, but he did not minimise the value of tongues when used properly. 'I would like every one of you to speak in another tongue' (14.5); 'I thank God that I speak in tongues more than you all' (14.18): these are not the comments of one who regards glossalalia as a triviality.

Paul referred both to 'speaking in tongues' and to 'praying in tongues'. It is not obvious that he had any distinction in mind, although nowadays 'speaking in tongues' usually refers to the exercise of this gift in public worship and 'praying in tongues' to its use in private devotion.

'If I pray in a tongue, my spirit prays, but my mind is unfruitful' (14.14). In terms of the apostle's psychology, the one who prays in a tongue is praying with his spirit rather than with his mind, and because he does not understand what he is saying, he does not gain any intellectual enlightenment from it. But that doesn't mean nothing is happening. He compressed into a few words a sequence of ideas: (1) that the Holy Spirit is at work in the believer, inspiring Christian worship and prayer; (2) that the work of the Spirit is crystallised into a specific gift — in this case, tongues; (3) that the gift is given in such personal terms that the believer can speak of it as his — 'his spirit' being the appropriate psychological channel through which the gift operates independently of his mind.

Speaking in tongues — or practices that seem to have been very much like it — have been experienced in most periods of the church's life. Some of the mystics in medieval times experienced speaking in tongues in their prayer. From the Reformation onwards revivalist groups, who turned to the scriptures for inspiration, sought and practised prayers and praises made up of unintelligible sounds which they believed constituted the same spiritual gift they read about in the New Testament.

What was distinctive about speaking in tongues in the Pentecostal revival at the beginning of this century was that it was regarded as evidence an individual had been 'baptised in the Spirit,' following the pattern of the accounts of the coming of the Spirit on groups of believers in Acts.

Within the charismatic renewal, speaking in tongues is valued as a form of private devotion. When we want to pray for someone, or to praise God freely, tongues provides us with a means of doing this without having to use our own language. We can fix our attention on the Lord, pray in tongues, and bring before him the persons or circumstances for whom we are interceding.

Of course, there is no means of proving that what

is called speaking in tongues today is exactly the same as what we read about in the New Testament. The distance between ourselves and the apostolic church in time and culture make it impossible to be certain. All I can say about it is that contemporary experiences of glossolalia, when discerningly exercised with gifts of interpretation, make much sense of what we read about in Acts and 1 Corinthians.

One misunderstanding is that those who pray in tongues lose control of themselves and are caught up in an emotional trip. This is not the experience of any glossolist I know. Although speaking and praying in tongues can sometimes lead to an emotional experience, this is also true of any form of devotion — singing a stirring hymn, for example. Praying in tongues is no more emotional than any other form of praying; and it is always under the control of the one who prays.

22. Is a gift of interpretation of tongues the same as a translation?

Interpretation is not a translation of what has been uttered in tongues, nor is it a commentary on it. Rather, it is a presentation in a known language of the content of what was said in tongues (which is why the interpretation may seem shorter or longer). It is as much a gift of the Spirit as speaking in tongues or any other charism, and it does not depend on an individual's skill in languages or literary expression.

The gift of interpretation may be given to the one who speaks in tongues or to others who listen to him. Old Testament charismatics like Joseph and Daniel had the gift of interpreting dreams: they pointed beyond the details of the dream to its message (Genesis 40.8; Daniel 2.3). The Greek *hermeneia* means an interpretation, an exposition, or an explanation. It converts what is unintelligible into what is intelligible.

Everything we know about the use of this gift in the apostolic church is in 1 Corinthians 12-14. Paul was writing to a church where, as we gather from elsewhere in this letter, the members were proud of the spiritual manifestations they experienced, and the apostle had to warn them about pride, counterfeit, and abusing the things of God. The indiscriminate use of tongues may have been a feature of the disorderly worship he had heard about in Corinth.

The gift of interpretation is always mentioned in relation to the gift of tongues and is complementary to it (1 Corinthians 12.10; 12.30; 14.5,13,28). It makes the gift of tongues meaningful when that charism is exercised publicly. Although Paul valued the gift as a means of building up the individual Christian, he directed that it should only be used in the presence of a congregation when a gift of interpretation was manifested as well: 'If anyone speaks in a tongue, two — or at the most three — should speak, one at a time, and someone must interpret. If there is no interpreter, the speaker should keep quiet in the church and speak to himself and to God' (14.27-28).

A good deal of 1 Corinthians 14 is occupied with the argument that tongues without interpretation is not edifying for a congregation and that the Lord is more likely to speak through a gift of prophecy. The apostle did not undervalue the gift of tongues. It was simply a matter of which charism was appropriate in the circumstances.

'I would like every one of you to speak in tongues, but I would rather have you prophesy. He who prophesies is greater than one who speaks in tongues, unless he interprets so that the church may be edified' (14.5); 'I thank God that I speak in tongues more than all of you. But in the church I would rather speak five intelligible words to instruct others than ten thousand words in a tongue' (14.18-19). When tongues was followed by an interpretation, then the words uttered were inspired like those spoken under the inspiration of a gift of prophecy. And what was said could be understood by all who were present.

To stress the futility of using tongues without an interpretation, Paul pointed out that if an unbeliever came into the assembly while everyone was speaking in tongues, he would not understand what was being said and he would conclude that the Christians were going crazy. Saying this, the apostle recalled Isaiah 28.11-12, 'Through men of strange tongues and through the lips of foreigners I will speak to this people, but even then they will not listen to me' (14.21). In its original context, the text referred to the foreign speech of the Assyrian invaders, and the prophet was warning of Judah's impending defeat; but Paul applied it to a totally different situation to reinforce his directives.

In Acts 2 those who heard the disciples speaking in tongues recognised different languages. At Corinth the languages were not recognised and gifts of interpretation were necessary. This corresponds with the experience of glossolalia today. Very rarely at a charismatic prayer meeting will a gift of tongues uttered aloud be recognised as a known language. In the vast majority of instances nothing will be understood unless a gift of interpretation follows.

It was said that among groups who are inexperienced or poorly led, much of what is said in 'interpretations' sounds little more than a re-hash of biblical phrases and concepts. But all beginners are liable to make mistakes and none of us can claim to be infallible. A start has to be made somewhere. Charismatic prayer groups should encourage their members to experiment (in the proper sense of that word) and yet also test rigorously all manifestations they receive and accept the guidance of their pastoral leaders in the local church. Certainly no individual or group should act on an interpretation (or, indeed, any similar verbal charism) unless it has been tested and confirmed in other ways.

In some congregations gifts of tongues and interpretations have been manifested within the normal Sunday worship. Usually these are permitted either during a period of silence after the ministry of the word (the Bible readings) or during the intercessions, where there is scope for spontaneous prayer.

Audibility is a problem in large buildings. One of the most satisfactory ways of dealing with this is for the person who wishes to speak to approach the worship leader and explain briefly what he or she wants to say. This gives the leader an opportunity of testing it. Then the 'interpreter' is allowed to use the microphone to deliver his message. Nevertheless, when an interpretation has been listened to and tested, it can be a powerful sign of God's presence and can often direct our attention to aspects of his will that we have neglected, forgotten or not known.

23. What is 'singing in the Spirit'?

Singing in the Spirit is when a group of worshippers

use the gift of tongues to praise God together, allowing themselves to sing their 'tongues' spontaneously.

When I have given a lead in this form of praise, I have begun by saying a few words in a 'tongue' quietly and then pitched it on a note. I nearly always find myself moving on to different notes as a tune emerges. By this time others around me have also begun to sing, using their 'tongues', and our voices merge in harmonies which are often quite beautiful. There is a control over the singing, like that of an unseen musical director, which is sensed by everybody. The harmonies rise and fall until they fade away as mysteriously as they have come.

Singing in the spirit often takes place during a liturgical celebration. For example, at a eucharist the singing of the *Sanctus* ('Holy, holy, holy'), or of a devotional hymn at the communion, are opportunities for the worshippers to extend their praise and thanksgiving in this way.

Singing in the Spirit may be followed by a gift of interpretation. I have been present when the interpretation has been offered in the form of a spontaneous song by one of the congregation. But usually it remains 'uninterpreted' as an act of corporate, spontaneous devotion.

The expression 'singing in the Spirit' comes from 1 Corinthians 14.15, 'I will be singing with my spirit, but I will also sing with my mind.' We cannot be sure that what we experience as singing in the Spirit in the worship of the charismatic renewal is the same as that to which Paul referred, but it seems quite likely. It is also possible that this is what he was referring to when he spoke of 'spiritual songs' (Ephesians 5.19; Colossians 3.16).

Whether or not 'Spirit' is written with a capital

'S' or a small 's' is immaterial. In the letters of Paul the 'spirit' is that part of our human nature which is responsive initially to the promptings of the Holy Spirit of God.

Students of Christian worship have long known that much of the music that accompanied the liturgy in the early centuries was improvised. Although certain forms of chanting the prayers and psalms were traditional — primitive plainchant which may have been derived from Jewish sources — much was left for leaders of worship and their congregations to make up their songs of praise using random speech sounds.

Since many of these worshippers were illiterate and hymn-books unknown, this was one of the ways in which congregations could join in joyful praise. It was known in Latin as *jubilatio*, a form of wordless singing which is familiar to historians of medieval music. It happened in a liturgical setting, for example, when 'Alleluia' was sung before the chanting of the gospel at the eucharist and the final 'a' led into a long and spontaneous wordless song, a practice related to improvisation in church music.

The word 'yodel' is derived from *jubilatio:* Alpine shepherds still call one another with this wordless singing.

The practice of singing in the Spirit is akin to what is known about *jubilatio*, making allowances for the differences in society and culture between the early medieval worshipper and ourselves. The Pentecostals were part of the continuing wave of revivalism that began in the eighteenth century with John Wesley and with the German pietists such as Count Zinzendorf who influenced Wesley.

In language, styles of prayer and emphasis on a change of heart, the Wesleys and the pietists had their roots in medieval Catholic groups. Writers such as Thomas á Kempis, Fenelon, and Madame Guyon had a profound influence on Wesley. Zinzendorf embraced Waldensian and Hussite teachings and practices whose styles of prayer, worship and language owed much to the medieval church. Through these influences medieval devotion to the name of Jesus and to the cross, and the medieval penchant for expressive worship and spiritual experiences, were passed on to the Weslyan revivalists and, from them, to the holiness movements of the nineteenth century, of which classical Pentecostalism was the most striking development.

Although *jubilatio* as such was not preserved through these later centuries, speaking in tongues was a feature of various revivals, and with it came a climate of language, a style of worship, and an expectancy of faith which characterises the modern renewal. Singing in the Spirit emerges out of this long history of praise from New Testament times through medieval Catholicism to the present day.

24. What is a gift of prophecy?

There is much misunderstanding about the gift of prophecy as it is manifested in charismatic circles. Some assume that prophecy is a form of inspired teaching; others that it is a delusion about hotlines to God and personal spiritual infallibility. Such misunderstanding, I might add, is nearly as common inside charismatic circles as outside them!

I will summarise the New Testament teaching on this gift in this answer and illustrate its contemporary relevance in the answer to the next question.

To prophesy is 'to proclaim' or 'to tell openly'

('to forth tell') — an exercise which may at the
same time throw light on the past, the present, or
the future. In the exercise of this spiritual gift, the
one who prophesies acts as a voice of God — 'the
voice of one calling in the desert' (John 1.23) was
the description of the prophetic forerunner. Such
voices can only proclaim or tell openly God's word
within the limitations of imperfect human response
and varying human cultures. Nevertheless, God
can still communicate with us through a gift of
prophecy by his Spirit within those limitations.

The gift of prophecy was manifested under the
old covenant, as God revealed himself to those
whom he had chosen to speak his word. In the
earliest period visions seemed to have played a
special role, for according to 1 Samuel 9.9, prophets
were originally called 'seers'. The sayings of the
major and minor prophets constitute about a third
of the Old Testament.

However, a distinction has to be made between
those who were called to be prophets and the gift of
prophecy. That is why the scriptures speak of both
prophets and prophesying. For example, it is said of
the seventy elders chosen by Moses to help him lead
the people: 'When the Spirit rested on them, they
prophesied, but they did not do so again' (Numbers
11.25). Their prophesying was a sign that God had
poured out his Spirit on them; but evidently this did
not mean they were called to be prophets.

Jesus himself exercised the gift of prophecy in
saying and doing only what he heard or saw from
the Father. 'The words that I say to you are not just
my own. Rather, it is the Father, living in me, who
is doing his work' (John 14.10). After Pentecost,
that prophetic gift which Jesus manifested would be
exercised by his disciples: 'The Spirit will take from

what is mine and make it known to you' (John 16.15).

The first disciples saw in their experiences after Pentecost the fulfilment of the prophecy of Joel about the 'last days': 'In the last days, God says, I will pour out my Spirit on all people. Your sons and daughters will prophesy, your young men will see visions, your old men will dream dreams. Even on my servants, both men and women, I will pour out my Spirit in those days, and they will prophesy' (Joel 3.1-2; Acts 2.16-18).

The prophetic gift was manifested in two ways, for the apostolic writers refer both (1) to prophets and (2) to those who prophesy without being called prophets and without any indication that they were marked out by a prophetic vocation.

1. Among the former were Agabus (Acts 11.28; 21.10) and the five 'prophets and teachers' at Antioch, including Barnabas and Saul (Acts 15.32). Luke also describes the aged widow Anna as a prophetess (Luke 2.36), and tells us that the evangelist Philip had four unmarried daughters who prophesied (Acts 21.9). Paul considered the prophets to be important members of the Christian community, for he put them second after 'apostles' in his list of ministries (1 Corinthians 12.28; Ephesians 2.20; 3.5; 4.11). In Ephesians the prophets were inspired to receive insights which they communicate as mediators to the church. In Acts they had a more practical task: predicting the famine that led to the organisation of relief among the Christians of Antioch for the churches of Judah (Acts 11.27-30); deciding, after prayer and fasting, that Saul and Barnabas should be sent out on a missionary journey (Acts 13.1-3); taking the decisions of the church in Jerusalem to the church in

Antioch (Acts 15.22-34).

2. Then there were also those who prophesied without being called prophets. These appear to have been individuals and groups who once or occasionally manifested the gift. Because they did not have a leading role in the community we can call this ministry 'congregational prophecy'. The twelve disciples of John the Baptist whom Paul baptised spoke in tongues and prophesied, though did not, as far as we know, become prophets (Acts 19.6). During Paul's last journey to Jerusalem he received prophecies from different congregations that imprisonment and affliction awaited him (Acts 20.23) The phrases used are: 'the Holy Spirit warns me' and 'the Holy Spirit says'. 'Through the Spirit they urged Paul not to go on to Jerusalem' refers to congregational prophecy (Acts 21.4).

The first reference to prophecy in 1 Corinthians strongly suggests Paul was speaking of congregational prophecy by women as well as men (1 Corinthians 11.4-5). This is confirmed by the apostle's discussion of prophecy in 1 Corinthians 14. In verse 1 of this chapter he exhorted the Corinthians, 'Eagerly desire spiritual gifts, especially the gift of prophecy.' Then he went on in verse 5, 'I would like every one of you to speak in tongues, but I would rather have you prophesy.' Not that he believed all of them would be prophets (1 Corinthians 12.29). Rather, he seems to have expected others to prophesy besides the prophets whom he named second to the apostles among those whom 'God has appointed in the church' (1 Corinthians 12.28). It is interesting to note that although Paul discusses this spiritual gift at length in 1 Corinthians, he nowhere names an individual prophet.

The gift of prophecy, then, is a work of the Holy Spirit among members of the Christian community. In some cases individuals are called by God to proclaim his word to that community or to individuals in it in particular circumstances. More widely, however, it is a gift of inspiration to the congregation as a whole which manifests itself through different members at different times. It is this second form of the charism, congregational prophecy, which is being experienced among some groups and communities in the contemporary renewal. Once this is understood, the manifestation of this particular gift is no longer an outlandish exercise but an extension of the ways in which the Lord has often spoken to his people through inspired individuals.

25. Is a gift of prophecy any use for today?

There have been many conferences and books on the church's pastoral strategy in recent decades; but few of them have considered what could be the role of the prophetic gifts. Which is remarkable when we look at the importance of those charisms in the mission of the New Testament church.

When we compare what Paul and Luke said about the function of prophecy in the Christian community, we notice that there are points of similarity and points of contrast. Whereas Luke stressed the notion of prophecy as a prediction of future events, by which people can be guided in the decisions they have to make, Paul nowhere mentioned prediction of the future as part of the prophecy. On the other hand, both Paul and Luke made use of the Greek verb *parakalein* and its cognate noun *parakalesis* in the same way to describe what prophecy is for.

It is difficult to translate the verb *parakalein* by just one English word: it can mean to encourage, to exhort, or to console. Likewise the noun *paraklesis* can mean encouragement, exhortation, or consolation. In one or other of these forms the word appears wherever those with a gift of prophecy address the people, e.g. 'with many other words John (the Baptist) exhorted the people' (Luke 3.18).

Luke translated the Aramaic name Barnabas, which the apostles conferred on the disciple Joseph, as 'Son of Encouragement', to show what his function was in the community (Acts 4.36). So when news of the spread of the gospel in Antioch reached the church in Jerusalem, they sent Barnabas there. 'When he arrived and saw the evidence of the grace of God, he was glad and encouraged them all to remain true to the Lord with all their hearts. He was a good man, full of the Holy Spirit and faith' (Acts 11.23-24). A little later Luke mentioned Barnabas first in his list of prophets and teachers at Antioch (Acts 13.1). A passage in Acts which demonstrates well the prophets' role is in 15.32: 'Judas and Silas, who themselves were prophets, said much to encourage and strengthen the brothers.'

In 1 Corinthians 14 Paul described the effects he expected prophecy to have on the congregation: 'Everyone who prophesies speaks to men for their strengthening, encouragement and comfort' (verse 3) and, 'You can all prophesy in turn so that everyone may be instructed and encouraged' (verse 31). The apostle apparently regarded prophecy as different from inspired preaching and teaching. The preacher or teacher had a spiritual gift which was with him all the time; he could use it whenever he wished. But the prophet could only prophesy when he was inspired to do so; and he could only do this when he believed that he was receiving from God a message to communicate. That is why elsewhere Paul urged, 'If a man's gift is prophesying, let him use it in proportion to his faith' (Romans 12.6).

Paul seemed to have been thinking of congregational prophecy in this passage rather than the ministry of the prophet, although the distinction may not have been as clearcut to him (see the answer to the previous question). He pointed out the need for orderliness in letting members exercise this gift: 'Two or three prophets should speak, and the others should weigh carefully what is said' (1 Corinthians 14.29).

Timothy was reminded of the prophecies which had been spoken to him when he received the laying on of hands with prayer (1 Timothy 1.18 and 4.14). Presumably it was not unlike the beginning of Paul's first mission: 'While they were worshipping the Lord and fasting, the Holy Spirit said, "Set apart for me Barnabas and Saul for the work to which I have called them"' (Acts 13.2). Gifts of prophecy, then, not only instructed and encouraged the congregations; they guided their decision-making processes.

The most outstanding Christian prophet in New Testament times was the author of the book of Revelation. He claimed that the words he received for the seven congregations in Asia Minor came from the Lord himself: 'On the Lord's Day I was in the Spirit, and I heard behind me a loud voice like a trumpet, which said, "Write on a scroll what you see and send it to the seven churches"' (Revelation 1.10-11). To be 'in the Spirit', a phrase used several times, is to be 'under inspiration', when the prophet 'hears' and 'sees' what God wants to communicate. Each letter is then presented to each particular church like Old Testament prophecies, as 'words of the Lord'; and each ends with the exhortation, 'He who has an ear, let him hear what the Spirit says to the churches' (2.7, 11, 29; 3.6, 13, 22).

To sum up, when we consider the enormous importance of the gift of prophecy in the apostolic church, it is difficult to believe that this charism — both in its individual and congregational forms — has been completely withdrawn by God from his people. Throughout this century the mainline denominations have been content to look back on one or two of their outstanding leaders as recent prophets (William Temple has been regarded as one in the years since his death in 1944) but have never expected prophetic gifts of a more simple kind to congregations to assist them in their mission now.

It was the Pentecostal churches which rediscovered this form of prophecy as they sought to restore the New Testament church in their own experience. They expected God to speak to them through prophetic utterances, and they believed that he did precisely that.

I came across this expectancy in a black Pentecostal church some years ago when I attended their anniversary celebrations. On the platform with the elders was a very old man who appeared to take no part in the proceedings. When I enquired who he was, I was told he was 'our prophet'. 'When we want to know what God wants us to do, he asks God for us and then tells us what God says,' one of the elders explained.

I gathered that the prophet has been

instrumental in helping that congregation to acquire the church building in which we were meeting. It had been declared redundant and had come on the market at a price far greater than the black congregation could hope to afford. However, the prophet had told them God was commanding them to buy the building, so they signed the contract and in an astonishing way the money was provided. I learned something about God's way of helping us in our decision-making processes that day!

Charismatics are trying to apply these lessons to their own lives, both individually and as members of communities and congregations.

I was once the recipient of a prophetic utterance given by an Indian preacher who did not even know my name or anything about me: he foretold the future shape of my ministry, and it was not until years later that I realised how truly he had spoken.

A community of which I was a member was told, through a prophecy, that every visitor who came to it would be blessed in a variety of ways; and that prophecy has been fulfilled many times over (remembering that to prophesy can mean to encourage and to exhort).

The congregation to which I belong now was given a prophecy during a prayer meeting to embark on a frighteningly expensive restoration scheme. The prophecy was written down and circulated to members of the parochial church council (a rigorous way of testing it!). Eventually the church council decided that what had been said was a word from the Lord and that they were to proceed with the plan. Years later the work was completed and paid for.

Prophecies today provide guidance, encouragement, and sometimes warnings, to Christians. They serve as a faith-building reminder that the Lord is Head of his church and that what we are to do is to listen to him and to obey him, trusting him for all that we require in order to fulfil his will. They also correct the current impression that the only manner in which decisions can be taken in the Christian community is through the majority votes of church councils or the opinions of experts.

26. Should we take every prophecy or interpretation of tongues we hear seriously?

The New Testament contains warnings about false prophecy. Jesus told his disciples, 'Watch out for false prophets. They come to you in sheep's clothing, but inwardly they are ferocious wolves' (Matthew 7.13). It is noteworthy that he expected them to exercise spiritual gifts and to perform miracles in his name (Matthew 7.22-23). 1 John was addressed to a church which was being troubled by false prophets: 'Dear friends, do not believe every spirit, but test the spirits to see whether they are from God, because many false prophets have gone out into the world' (1 John 4.1).

In Paul's list of spiritual gifts, 'distinguishing between spirits' comes after 'prophecy' (1 Corinthians 12.10). He mentioned it later in the letter (14.29) and also in an earlier writing (1 Thessalonians 5.19-22). The Greek word he used *diakrisis* means 'to weigh'. The gift is therefore an anointing of the Spirit which enables individuals and congregations to evaluate, to investigate and to test both the source of the inspired utterance and its significance for the congregation.

The New Testament writers agree that there are

two criteria for distinguishing between true and false prophets: the moral character of the prophet and the orthodoxy of his messages. 'By their fruit you will recognise them' (Matthew 7.16). The false prophet Jezebel was denounced for her immorality (Revelation 2.20-21). Orthodox teaching about Jesus is the test which 1 John puts forward for discerning between the true and the false prophet: 'Every spirit that acknowledges that Jesus Christ has come in the flesh is from God' (1 John 4.2-3). Paul also taught that what a person says about Jesus shows by what sort of a spirit he is inspired (1 Corinthians 12.3).

When applied to our experiences of charisms in the renewal today, these lessons suggest that when we hear interpretations and prophecies which seem to be addressed to us or to the group or congregation of which we are members, we should ask certain questions:

1. What do we think of the person who made the prophecy or gave the interpretation? Did he strike us as a man of God? In answering this question, bear in mind our Lord's warning I have just quoted: that the exercise of remarkable spiritual gifts does not in itself mean that the one who ministers is always his disciple.

2. Was the prophecy (or interpretation of tongues) in harmony with what we know of God's nature and will from the scriptures? That doesn't necessarily mean we have to find a text somewhere in the Bible to fit in with it. Rather, it means we have to decide whether or not it reflected God, the Father, the Son, and the Holy Spirit, as revealed to us through his word.

3. Did the prophecy conflict in any way with the teaching of the Christian church? Of course, in

some matters, the church has not always spoken with a united voice. Nevertheless, over a wide range of doctrinal and moral issues there is a general concensus of Christian thought which can guide us in responding to prophecies and interpretations.

4. Have we shared the prophecy with other Christians, especially those who are also wise in the faith and those who exercise pastoral leadership in the church? The New Testament has much to say about ministering in pairs and seeking the advice of two or three fellow disciples. It also shows that spiritual gifts of leadership are given to guard the flock of Christ from harm.

5. Using what we might call sanctified common sense, do we feel that the prophecy was likely to come from the Lord, bearing in mind our present situation?

6. If the prophecy included a specific direction to us, concerning our relationships with particular persons or our future, have we received anything which confirms what was said from other, independent sources? We would be very unwise to take some important step in our life (like, say, resigning a job) just on a word given in a charismatic prayer meeting. We ought to ask the Lord to give us confirmation of such a step in other ways before we take it seriously.

Prophecies and interpretations can be powerful encouragements and guides to us when they are properly discerned and tested; but if they are false, they can cause havoc in the lives of individuals, communities and congregations.

27. How do you know when you should speak an interpretation or prophecy, and what do you do about it?

There is no set formula to show how individuals respond to these gifts, but the following experiences seem to be fairly common.

During worship or prayer with others, a thought comes into your mind which persists even if you try to forget it. The thought may consist of just one word, or a few words, or perhaps a picture. Sometimes a whole message is revealed.

When this happens, you consider it for a while. You don't rush in right away. You examine it and offer it back to God, praying that if you are to speak the interpretation or the prophecy, an opportunity will be given. The persistence of the thought may be an indication that you are being moved by the Holy Spirit to speak out in Jesus' name.

You may have to wait for a while until an appropriate moment comes in the worship or prayer group. In a large meeting it may be necessary to go to whoever is leading and tell him what you feel the Lord is pressing you to say. He will then give you an opportunity to speak to the meeting (but if he tells you he doesn't think it is suitable, accept his decision without an argument). In a small meeting, like a prayer group, you don't normally have to seek permission.

Once the appropriate moment arrives, you have to take the risk in faith and speak out the phrase or the sentence, trusting the Spirit to give you the rest. The extent to which you have to trust God in this can be quite daunting. But this in itself is a good check: you wouldn't dare to say it unless you had some awareness that it was the Lord's inspiration, not your invention!

When you have started, be ready for the inner nudge to stop. Don't be tempted to elaborate or to make things up if you feel the inspiration is leaving you. Be as simple as you can.

You may see a picture in your mind, or you may recall a dream you had recently, with a strong impression that it conveys a message to someone who is present. Again, be simple and don't attempt to interpret what you describe. Let the Spirit do the interpreting in the minds of those who are listening to you.

Those who prophesy are not always aware that they are doing so. During a sermon, for example, a preacher may receive a prophetic anointing so that he is led to speak with unusual power and authority things which he had not prepared in his notes.

Overall this sense of anointing is usually important. It can come in various ways — a deep conviction which is not just an emotional reaction, or a peculiar physical tension. There are no guaranteed signs, but those who are used in the ministry of prophecy gradually learn to recognise the promptings of the Spirit.

If possible, respond to this gift in a small group among those who know you. Be humble about it, and encourage them to be honest with you in reviewing what you've said. Don't be fearful of making mistakes — and don't be touchy about straightforward comments. Be yourself. Don't search for memorable or scriptural-sounding phrases. Just say what you feel the Lord wants you to say — and then shut up.

It's pretentious to preface your words with 'thus saith the Lord'. Let others discern whether or not those words are really of God. The best way of introducing a prophecy or an interpretation is to be relaxed within yourself, look around at the others, and begin by saying, 'I think the Lord may be saying this to us....'

I have met some groups who kept notes of what was prophesied at their meetings. The notes can make fascinating and encouraging reading years later. One group I visited had a cassette player handy to switch on whenever anyone believed they had a gift of prophecy.

At large charismatic gatherings, recordings are often made of interpretations and prophecies given during the main meetings, and a selection of these are sometimes published along with the reports drawn up afterwards.

GIFTS AND MINISTRIES

28. What do charismatics mean when they talk about 'an every member ministry'?

The gifts of the Holy Spirit are bestowed on the people of God in order to equip them to say and do the things that the Lord wants them to do to serve him. This is obvious if we consider the effects of spiritual gifts — prophecy, powerful teaching, evangelism, leadership, teaching, administration. They are all concerned with enabling the church to be an instrument of the gospel in today's world. Although some charisms may seem highly personal, like praying in tongues privately, nevertheless the ultimate result should be that the individual who prays is better equipped to serve God among others.

It is this concept of service which is at the root of the word 'ministry'. We have a rather limited view of what ministry means because we tend to associate it exclusively with those who are ordained to pastoral leadership in the church ('going into the ministry'). But the biblical teaching is that every Christian is baptised in the Holy Spirit in order to be a servant of God.

Let us look at a 'service' we are all familiar with — an act of worship in church. When we assemble as a congregation, we all participate in worship, either individually or corporately, and in this way we minister to, or perform a service for, God the Father through our union with his Son Jesus Christ in the power of the Holy Spirit. But our service for God is not temporarily suspended when we leave the church. It continues in all we do from one act of worship to the next. We serve God by engaging in those services for others to which he calls us.

After his great exposition of the saving act of God

in Jesus Christ and the gift of the Holy Spirit, Paul wrote, 'Therefore, I urge you, brothers, in view of God's mercy, to offer your bodies as living sacrifices, holy and pleasing to God — this is your spiritual act of worship' (Romans 12.1). He used the phrase 'spiritual act of worship' to emphasise that what we say and do as God's servants is something quite different from the forms of sacrifice experienced in contemporary pagan temples.

In the last hundred years there has been a gradual recovery of what is usually known as 'the ministry of the laity', especially in those denominations which tend to be dominated by the ordained clergy. This has shown itself in a variety of ways — in the greater role taken by the laity in church government at national as well as local levels, in the many lay training schemes which are available, and in the increase in the number of church posts which are open to those who are not ordained.

The emphasis on training and qualifications mirrors the secular educational world — and, indeed, some of the lay training is done within the secular educational structures, like the extra-mural departments of universities and the extension studies offered by theological colleges and Christian institutes. There is much talk about 'the lay apostolate' and 'laity development'.

The lesson which the charismatic renewal has underlined is that what we do as God's servants can only be done in the power of his Holy Spirit. Training for theological qualifications may be right for certain lay ministries as it is for ordained ministries; but in the end we serve God, not because of our academic qualifications, but because he anoints us with his Spirit and equips us with spiritual gifts to fulfil his purpose.

The renewal is doing much to help churches realise that lay women and men can minister to God and serve one another by leading worship, praying for healing, prophesying, and evangelising, as well as by offering hospitality, administering the finances, and doing the less public jobs which surround any Christian congregation.

'Each one should use whatever gift he has received to serve others, faithfully administering God's grace in its various forms' (1 Peter 4.10). For nearly all of us that ministry begins in our own homes, where we need God's grace — his spiritual gifts — to be good wives and husbands, mothers and fathers, daughters and sons, sisters and brothers, friends and neighbours. We need God's grace, too, in our work and leisure situations — both to go about those activities and relationships as God's servant in all that we do, and also to receive spiritual gifts for particular situations — perhaps a word of knowledge in helping someone who seeks our advice, or the charism of an evangelist when someone else asks us about our faith.

This growing appreciation of the true function of spiritual gifts has led to the use of the phrase 'every member ministry'. It means assisting every Christian in a congregation to have a greater trust that God can and will use them for his purpose by the power of his Holy Spirit in Jesus' name wherever they are.

29. Do I need my vicar's/pastor's permission before I engage in any ministry?

It depends on the situation. Obviously if you are acting in a private capacity — if, say, one of your family is ill at home and you feel it is right to pray

with them for healing with the laying on of hands —
then there is no need to consult your vicar or pastor.
You may wish to consult him later if particular
difficulties arise, or if you want him to bring the
patient communion. But in general what you do in
your own home or among your circle of friends is
your affair.

However, when you begin to minister in a
situation where you are not acting in a private
capacity, then other considerations arise. What you
do publicly could be seen as in some way represent-
ing the church of which you are a member, and
therefore that congregation is involved in what you
say and do. For example, if you spontaneously pray
with someone for healing in a public meeting and as
a result something goes wrong, your vicar and
congregation might be drawn into the trouble and
you may put them in an embarrassing or controver-
sial position.

Certain ministries exercised in public should
never be undertaken, except in rare and extreme
cases, without your pastor's permission. The ministry of deliverance is one of these. So also are forms
of preaching or teaching in which you are acting as
a representative of the congregation of which you
are a member.

This is not an encouragement for authoritarian
leadership or ecclesiastical bureaucracy. It is
simply a wise precaution and an acknowledgement
that when we minister in Jesus' name we do so as
members of the Christian community — with all
the responsibilities as well as the privileges that
such membership entails. To respect the pastoral
leadership of our congregation is one of these
responsibilities.

Once your vicar knows you are likely to be

involved in any ministry, he can do much to
support and encourage you. Not only will he give
you advice but he will also be prepared if there is
any comeback which he has to deal with. Furthermore, if that ministry develops, he will arrange
for you to be trained or to work alongside others
with more experience.

Once your ministry — whatever it is — has come
to be recognised and accepted by your church, then
prior consultation is not so necessary. The
denominations have different ways of authorising
charismatic ministries. In some Anglican dioceses
lay persons are commissioned by the parish priest
or by the bishop for local ministries. Other
denominations have more informal arrangements.

Even so, it is vital that those who exercise these
local ministries keep in touch with their pastor, for
they are engaging in various forms of shared
leadership, and that means a close partnership with
each other in the Lord. It is also vital that those
engaged in ministries beyond the congregation
should keep in touch with their base.

The pastor of an independent congregation I
know was gradually led to accept invitations to
participate in evangelistic missions both in this
country and overseas. He was clearly being led into
the ministry of an evangelist, and his congregation,
recognising this, appointed an assistant pastor to
lead them when he was away.

He discussed this development with me one day,
and I pointed out to him that this was the sort of
situation in which the pastor who is increasingly
absent from his congregation one day returns to
find he has been replaced by his assistant. In
extreme cases, he is then without a job! I suggested
he made an arrangement with the congregation

that he was not away more than a certain number of weeks a year, that he took groups with him on missions when it was possible, and that he reported back to the congregation both when he was away by letter and when he returned so that they all felt involved in what he undertook.

Years later, as his ministry extended, he told me he had followed these suggestions and he had never experienced any difficulty in relating either to the congregation or to the assistant pastor.

If we believe we are the body of Christ, with each member exercising different ministries, but all needing the ministries of others, then the kind of things I have described are necessary practical steps for maintaining the church's unity and forwarding her mission.

30. What is the connection between ordination and spiritual gifts?

Ordination means conferring authority on a man (or a woman, in some denominations) to exercise pastoral leadership in the church. Although ordination in the first instance is usually linked with an appointment to a particular congregation, the authorisation is recognised throughout the denomination. This means that when the ordained pastor moves to another congregation, he doesn't have to be re-ordained.

The pastor presides over the congregation, guiding it as it seeks God's purposes for it. Pastors are, in their turn, presided over by a bishop or an equivalent (Methodist chairman of district, United Reformed provincial moderator, etc.) who in his office represents the unity of the wider church in Jesus Christ.

From the New Testament we learn that only those called by God can exercise the authority of a leader; and that those God calls are equipped by his Spirit to fulfil that ministry of leadership. This call has to be discerned by the church through its existing apostles and leaders; then the church authorises those who were called through prayer for the Holy Spirit and the laying on of hands before sending them on the mission or task to which God was calling them. When they were appointed within existing congregations, those leaders were often the older men (presbyters, elders) in the community.

In Acts there are various occasions when men were authorised through prayer and the laying on of hands, laying down a pattern for future ordinations in the church. Seven men 'full of the Holy Spirit and wisdom' were 'ordained' to assist the apostles (6.1-6); Paul and Barnabas were 'ordained' for the missionary journey they were undertaking (13.1-3); Paul spoke to the elders in Ephesus, reminding them they had been given the gift of the Holy Spirit for the ministry of oversight of God's flock (20.28).

Congregations were exhorted to obey their pastoral leaders because these men had been called and authorised to care for them by God himself. 'Respect those who work hard among you, who are over you in the Lord and who admonish you. Hold them in the highest regard in love because of their work' (1 Thessalonians 5.12-13). 'Obey your leaders and submit to their authority. They keep watch over you as men who must give an account. Obey them so that their work will be a joy' (Hebrews 13.17).

The precise nature of the ordained ministry is a

matter which has divided Christians in the past, although there are signs that in recent years their views are converging. All major denominations now agree that ordination consists of the following essential elements:

1. A call by God
2. The willingness of the one called to respond in obedience.
3. The discernment of that call by the Christian community (together with training).
4. The authorisation of the one called, by prayer with the laying on of hands, for the gifts of the Holy Spirit to enable him to fulfil that ministry.
5. The sending or placing of the one ordained in the congregation for the task for which he is selected (in Anglican terms, 'a title').

The gifts of the Spirit, then, are as necessary for the pastoral leadership as they are for members of a congregation. But because leadership is a vital ministry in the church, the calling and ordination of pastors is a regulated process in all denominations, and in that process the discernment of the charism of leadership is an essential part.

This is demonstrated in the ordination services used throughout the church. In a service presided over by a bishop, the candidates are first presented to the bishop who formally examines them about their own response to God's call (he has, of course, conducted this examination informally during the months beforehand):

> *Do you believe, so far as you know your own heart, that God has called you to the office and work of a priest in his church?*

After further questions he asks them:

> *Will you in the strength of the Holy Spirit continually stir up*

the gift of God that is in you, to make Christ known to all men?

Then he presents them to the congregation, asking for their approval of the candidates and their willingness to uphold them in their ministry. After this comes the prayers for the Holy Spirit and the laying on of hands. In this way, the traditional liturgy enshrines the biblical pattern of discerning and authorising those with spiritual gifts of pastoral leadership.

But what happens if a man gradually loses the charism of leadership while he holds a leadership post in the church, and decides to change to some other ministry?

Ordination by itself does not qualify a man to be a vicar or a pastor. He also has to be licensed or accredited to be appointed to a post. A priest in the Anglican church, for example, has to receive a fresh licence from his bishop before he can become the vicar of a parish. And if a vicar or pastor ceases to exercise a leadership role in a congregation — through persistent neglect or gross scandal — denominations have processes which enable them to dismiss him or persuade him to resign.

31. Isn't the ministry of deliverance just a return to medieval superstition?

In the Lord's Prayer we ask God to 'deliver us from evil' or, 'from the evil one' (it could mean both). The experience of the first Christians was that through Jesus Christ, God had delivered them from the grip of evil and brought them into the realm of light. 'He has rescued us from the dominion of darkness and brought us into the kingdom of the Son he loves, in whom we have redemption, the forgiveness of sins' (Colossians 1.13). The healings of Christ, which sometimes involved the casting out of evil spirits, were recognised as powerful manifestations of God's kingdom breaking through into this life.

Exorcism, or casting out of evil, has been an important ministry of the church from New Testament times. It became a standard element in the rites of Christian initiation. Even today, when anyone is baptised, the liturgies require the candidate to renounce evil, and in the Roman Catholic and Orthodox traditions the candidate is anointed with the oil of exorcism. Many bishops appoint exorcists from among their clergy who are experienced in the ministry of deliverance.

Alongside this we have to recognise that some modern Christians deny the existence of Satan and attribute all forms of evil to the circumstances in which we live — rebellious and aggressive impulses within ourselves individually and corporately, the effects of our upbringing, relationships and environment, and the outcome of things that happen around us by chance or misfortune.

This is an enormous question which I cannot discuss here. All I can say is that, as many Christians become more aware of the Holy Spirit's presence and power, they also become more aware of the presence and power of the evil one. While much wickedness is no doubt due to our human failings, yet we occasionally discern in human rebellion against the goodness of God a wicked force which is not explained just in terms of personal weakness or tragic happenings. The devil becomes very real and the biblical warnings become very relevant. His influence has to be cast out in Jesus' name. That constitutes the ministry of deliverance.

Two further things about it should be said.

1. It is an extremely effective ministry when the need has been correctly discerned. Individuals have found themselves freed from all kinds of bondages when they have confessed their sins and submitted humbly to the deliverance God ministers to them through others. The prayer often includes a command to the evil spirit to depart from the individual, invoking the authority of Jesus and the power of Christ's sacrifice on the cross.

2. On the other hand, it is an extremely dangerous ministry for those who attempt to exercise it without being fully aware of what they are doing. For this reason it should never be attempted unless there is very clear evidence through a spiritual gift of discernment (mentioned by Paul in his list in 1 Corinthians 12.10) and all possible steps are taken to safeguard those involved. The ministry of deliverance engages us in a form of spiritual warfare which we should take as seriously as physical warfare.

For this reason, most denominations issue instructions on how this ministry is to be undertaken by their members; and these instructions include the following points:

a. Only minister in groups, preferably in a church building.

b. If possible, seek permission beforehand from, and always report afterwards to, the appropriate pastoral leadership (vicar, pastor, or — in the case of an ordained minister — a bishop or other senior church leader).

c. Involve someone who has had previous experience of this ministry.

d. Make time for preliminary counselling and seek medical advice (much damage has been done through attempting to 'deliver' patients whose real trouble was psychological).

e. Prepare all concerned spiritually for the ministry with prayer and, if possible, fasting. This preparation should include the client.

f. Be in control of the time and the place for this ministry. Don't be rushed into it because of apparent 'emergencies' (it is a well-known trick of an enemy to catch us off our guard).

g. Don't spend too long on it. All-night sessions and suchlike are unnecessary. If nothing seems to have happened, say, within an hour, postpone further ministry until another occasion.

h. After the ministry, make sure the client is incorporated into a Christian fellowship for after-care, until he or she is completely free from whatever it was that troubled them.

A final word. Never go looking for devils, but if your suspicions are roused, seek wise advice before raising the question with the person concerned.

32. What are words of wisdom and words of knowledge?

These spiritual gifts are among the nine listed by Paul in 1 Corinthians 12.7-11.

A word of wisdom is a gift which reflects God's will in the situations in which we find ourselves. Isaiah 11.2 prophesied that the Spirit of wisdom would rest on the Messiah, and we read in Luke 2.40 that Jesus was filled with wisdom. This is not human wisdom but the wisdom of God. Wisdom in its fullest sense belongs to God alone. It refers not only to the complete knowledge he has of all that he has created, but also to his ability to see how everything he wills is to be fulfilled. The fear of the

Lord, according to the Old Testament, is where we are to begin if we seek this gift.

Jesus exercised this charism on many occasions. Two examples are when he silenced his opponents about paying Caesar what was owed (Matthew 22.21) and when he directed the rich young man to sell all he had in order to become a disciple (Luke 18.22). He promised his followers words from the Spirit at critical moments: 'Whenever you are arrested and brought to trial, do not worry beforehand about what to say. Just say whatever is given you at the time, for it is not you speaking, but the Holy Spirit' (Mark 13.11). The gift was demonstrated in the apostles' defence of the gospel before the courts (Acts 4.19-20) and in the practical arrangements they made when tensions arose between the Hebrew and Hellenist Christians (Acts 6.3-4).

We need this charism in numerous daily situations. In family life, in church affairs, in business, and in all kinds of personal relationships, we are constantly placed in a position where we have to make decisions or to give opinions and advice which require God's guidance. If we are learning to be open to the Holy Spirit, we shall find ourselves led to saying things which, in retrospect, seem far beyond what we are able to think out for ourselves.

The way to exercise this spiritual gift is to try and set aside our uncertainties or fears about what we might be called on to say, and to trust the Lord. If we restrain ourselves from giving an immediate off-the-cuff answer, and if we offer a brief arrow prayer, words will be given us that meet the situation exactly. The sign of the spiritual gift is when, as a result, the situation is moved forward in accordance with God's will.

The word of knowledge is parallel to the word of wisdom. In this case, however, what is manifested is not God's will but divine insight. It is a gift through which there is revealed to us a knowledge of a person or a circumstance which is beyond our human reasoning. It could be likened to a very vivid and accurate intuition.

The charism is experienced in ministries such as counselling and preaching. Jesus had a word of knowledge when he was talking to the woman at the well in Samaria: although she was a stranger, he knew of her immorality (John 3.18). When writing to the church in Ephesus Paul had a word of knowledge on what he should teach them (Ephesians 3.1ff).

It is similar today. In a prayer counselling ministry, the one who listens to and prays with someone with a problem will be given an insight which does much to make that ministry a blessing. I have experienced this kind of help on various occasions when I have asked friends to pray with me about particular problems.

And in preparing to preach a sermon in church or giving a talk at a conference, I have sometimes had a strong impression — almost like a word spoken in my ear — that I should abandon what I had planned and take another topic, frequently linked with a passage of scripture. When I have done that, the result has often been very fruitful.

Because these gifts are closely related to natural abilities such as prudent judgement, solid teaching or powerful preaching, they are usually overlooked. They are called 'words of' because the gift is not manifested unless words are spoken to a specific person or situation. They differ from the gift of prophecy in that the latter brings a message directly from God and deals with matters which are totally unknown to the person using the gift.

33. Why do we hear so much about 'signs and wonders' these days?

The overall purpose of spiritual gifts is the edification of the church. But when the church is exercising ministries in the power of the Spirit, then it is also demonstrating the power of God's kingdom to the world. In Acts Peter reminded the crowd in Jerusalem on the day of Pentecost of the many signs and wonders they had seen in the ministry of Jesus, 'which God did among you through him' (2.22).

Then, as the mission of the church proceeded, further signs and wonders were seen (2.43) — the healing of the cripple (3.1-10), the punishment of Ananias and Sapphira (5.1-12), the ministry of Philip (8.13), and the mission of Paul and Barnabas at Iconium (14.3). When they were threatened with persecution, the church prayed: 'Stretch out your hand to heal and perform miraculous signs and wonders through the name of your holy servant Jesus' (4.30).

Paul pointed out that even a gift like prophesying has a 'sign and wonder' value, for the unbeliever who comes into a congregation which is exercising this gift will be convicted of his sin and will 'fall down and worship God, exclaiming, "God is really among you"' (1 Corinthians 14.24-25). Mark lists 'tongues' as a sign that would manifest itself among believers along with healing, exorcism, and power over poisons and serpents (Mark 16.17-18).

These New Testament teachings and experiences have been accepted wholeheartedly by certain

Christian groups in the twentieth century. The classical Pentecostals, for example, have majored on mass evangelistic healing crusades featuring the exercise of spiritual gifts. Although these crusades have met with limited success in the USA and Britain, they have been an important means of evangelising in some third-world countries. Crusades of this kind have led tens of thousands to Christ.

A striking example is the story told years ago of Alexander Abala of Zaire. As a boy he was brought up in an evangelical school in Zaire where he was taught that spiritual gifts had ceased after New Testament times. Because this teaching was so contrary to what he read in the Bible, he lost his faith and led a life of crime. A few years later he saw a poster advertising a tent meeting led by a well-known healing evangelist, T.L.Osborn, and he was determined to expose the man as a fraud. Taking a blind woman and several other friends to the service, he planned to expose the evangelist when the woman was not healed. To his utter astonishment, the woman was healed instantly. After this, Abala and his friends were converted and called into evangelistic ministries themselves. Abala and his followers planted over three thousand churches in Zaire, of the Pentecostal variety.

One of the current examples of 'power evangelism' is in the ministry of Reinhard Bonnke in Africa. His tent, which seats 34,000 people, is often too small to hold the crowds that are attracted to his services. He has preached to crowds estimated at 500,000 in Nigeria and other nations. The experiences of healing at these meetings have led thousands of Muslims to convert to Christianity.

Following the charismatic renewal, Christians in the older denominations have a confidence that God can act in power among them for his kingdom. As a result, the phrase 'signs and wonders' is frequently used when referring to ministries of healing and deliverance in the context of evangelistic and revivalist gatherings.

This form of mission has become well known through John Wimber's Vineyard Ministries in the USA, in Britain, and in other parts of the world, and it is gradually being applied in some congregations belonging to the older denominations where the charismatic renewal has been influential.

Although patterns vary, quite often this ministry of healing begins as a congregation is worshipping when the leader or the preacher invites everyone to join in a time of prayer. Then he has 'words of knowledge' that there is a certain person present who has a specified illness or disability, or who is suffering in some way; he continues, either by declaring that the person is being healed, or that he or she comes forward for the laying on of hands.

Like every other ministry, it has been accompanied by blessings and failures. Some have claimed remarkable healings; others have claimed the whole set-up was deceitful. I once took a doctor friend to a large 'signs and wonders' rally where three people came forward for the laying on of hands. They said they were healed there and then, but my friend was not convinced. Perhaps they were mistaken, or perhaps my friend was too sceptical to be impartial. I don't know.

It is dangerous when individuals and groups start seeking signs and wonders for their own sake, hoping to prove something about God for themselves or their more sceptical friends. Jesus warned

the crowds, 'This is a wicked generation. It asks for
a miraculous sign, but none will be given it except
the sign of Jonah' (Luke 11.29) — meaning a call to
repentance. He was prepared to heal the sick and to
drive out demons, and these miracles drew attention to the gospel he proclaimed; but he expected
his disciples to believe in him, not because of the
wonders they had seen, but because of the truth of
that gospel (John 6.26).

'Signs and wonders' is causing much discussion
and controversy in the church and people too easily
take sides for or against. A more mature attitude is
to learn from it that we should be prepared to take
risks for the Gospel, trusting that God will work
'signs and wonders' if he wishes to in his sovereign
power. But we should beware of falling into the trap
of trying to manipulate divine power.

That was the sin of Simon Magus, who offered
the apostles money if they would lay hands on him
to give him the power of the Spirit (Acts 8.18 - 19).
He failed to recognise that the initiative and the
sovereignty always belong to God alone. We can
only serve God and others if we are utterly humble
about this, putting the Lord first in everything.
Paul has given us an example: 'Therefore I glory in
Christ Jesus in my service to God. I will not venture
to speak of anything except what Christ has
accomplished through me in leading the Gentiles to
obey God by what I have said and done — by the
power of signs and miracles, through the power of
the Spirit' (Romans 15. 17-19).

34. Why did Paul speak of faith as a spiritual gift? Don't we all need to have faith?

Yes, we certainly all need 'saving faith'. This is the

faith which is the possession of every Christian; it is the basis of our discipleship, a complete trust in Jesus Christ as our Saviour and Lord. It is the faith which comes through hearing the message of the Gospel (Romans 10.17) and which expresses itself through how we live (James 2.17).

Closely associated with saving faith is faithfulness, a fruit of the Spirit (Galatians 5.22). This faithfulness grows within us through the Spirit's presence and produces a trustworthiness and reliability in the things of God, particularly in our dealing with others in Jesus' name.

But when he included 'faith by the same Spirit' in his list of spiritual gifts (1 Corinthians 12.9), the apostle seems to have been referring to a special charism bestowed on Christians in extraordinary circumstances. It is the faith to move mountains, a supernatural conviction that God will reveal his power, righteousness and mercy in a specific case.

When he receives this spiritual gift, the Christian is enabled, without any human reasoning or sense of doubt, to ask or to speak in the name of Jesus in such a way that what he says or asks must come to pass — for God, who inspires the Christian with such faith, will necessarily grant what he asks.

Many of the gospel events reflect this gift of faith in Jesus himself. One of the most striking examples was at the raising of Lazarus, when Jesus prayed, 'Father, I thank you that you have heard me. I know that you always hear me' (John 11.41-42). Peter received a similar gift at the gate of the temple when he healed the crippled man (Acts 3.16).

In modern times we recognise this charism in women and men who risk their freedom and their lives for the sake of the gospel. In Africa, in various Asian countries, and in Communist states in recent

decades, many Christians — particularly black and
coloured — have faced imprisonment and martyr-
dom because of their discipleship. Hearing their
stories, we are amazed and humbled at the extraordinary courage they showed. What amazed and
humbled us were spiritual gifts which endowed
them with a confidence far more than saving faith.

To a lesser extent we recognise it also in those
who are called by God to undertake tasks which
mean they have to step outside the normal secur-
ities which our church and society offer us. A few of
my friends have, in response to the Lord, resigned
from their jobs, sold their homes, and embarked on
ministries in which they depended entirely on what
God provided through the generosity of others.
They had gifts of faith which enabled them to do
more than is normally expected of Christians in
ordinary homes, jobs and congregations.

Often such charisms arise out of lives which have
been faithful over a number of years; but the same
gifts have been manifested in those who are quite
young Christians. It is important for the latter
especially to be discerning what the Lord's will for
them really is. Youthful enthusiasm for embarking
on 'faith missions' is not always the same as gifts of
faith.

Associated with these gifts is another charism
which Paul lists, 'miraculous powers' (1 Corinthians 12.10). These are remarkable events which
happen in response to prayer and which cannot be
explained through scientific or other means in the
life of the Christian and of the church. Since Paul
mentioned 'gifts of healing by that one Spirit' just
before this in his list (1 Corinthians 12.9), he was
presumably referring to other kinds of miraculous
happenings such as his own experiences of being

saved from shipwreck (Acts 27.44 - 28.1).

While the life of the average Christian might not be quite as dangerous as that, nevertheless if we are seeking to follow the Lord we shall from time to time experience extraordinary 'coincidences' or unexpected events which are not satisfactorily explained in terms of 'chance'. It is as if God takes hold of our lives and our circumstances in such a way that his purpose and power are revealed in a manner that can only be described as miraculous.

GIFTS OF HEALING

35. Can anyone pray for healing?

The straightforward answer is, yes, but we must relate that answer to the circumstances within which Christians pray for healing.

The most obvious circumstance is when we pray in our own homes. A mother prays for a sick child; a friend asks the Lord to heal us when an illness strikes us or when we are the victims of an accident. This is the simplest form of the ministry of healing, and sometimes we shall witness a gift of healing as a result.

Another circumstance is when we find ourselves led to pray for healing in informal situations like house groups and weekend conferences. Usually this happens when we are taking a lead in the proceedings or when we are invited to pray for healing by the one who is leading. Again, gifts of healing may be manifested.

Then there are the more formal services of prayer for healing which are now a feature of the regular worship in an increasing number of churches. Prayer and the laying on of hands in these circumstances is usually offered by the clergy, ministers and lay leaders in the congregation, who have had some training and preparation for the ministry.

Finally there are the Christian communities and groups who exercise a healing ministry and counsel those who come to them for advice, inner healing and deliverance from evil influences. Usually these communities and groups engage in this ministry with the co-operation of friends in the medical profession.

As we look down this table of circumstances, we shall note that there is an increasing degree of

specialisation by those who take part, and this is
why I feel my answer to the question has to be
qualified. To say that anyone can pray for healing is
not the same as saying that anyone should expect to
be able to exercise a ministry of healing in all
circumstances. Like other ministries, the gift of
healing is an act of the Holy Spirit in and through
the body of Christ. And those who are called on to
exercise this ministry within the church should be
prepared to do so only under the pastoral leadership of the congregation.

The New Testament does not refer to any
'healer', only to 'gifts of healing'. Jesus Christ is the
Healer of the new covenant, and all gifts of healing
are discerned as an act of the risen Lord through his
followers: 'The Lord worked with them and confirmed his word by the signs that accompanied it'
(Mark 16.20). The apostles invoked the gift of
healing in the name of Christ, as Peter did when he
met the crippled man at the temple gate called
Beautiful: 'In the name of Jesus Christ of Nazareth,
walk' (Acts 3.6).

Yet it is a fact of Christian experience throughout
the ages that certain individuals exercise this
charism more than others — some to the extent that
they might be called 'specialists'. One of the most
famous in England at the beginning of the century
was James Moore Hickson who founded the Divine
Healing Mission. Hickson was a lay member of the
Church of England whose healing ministry eventually took him all over the world. Other Anglicans
were Dorothy Kerin, who founded the Burrswood
home of healing, and Canon George Bennet of
Coventry. But none of them would have claimed to
be a 'healer'. Their only claim was that they
attempted to be obedient servants of God who
heals.

36. Is it always necessary to lay on hands and/or anoint when we pray with another for healing?

When Jesus healed, he frequently touched the sick, like the leper (Matthew 8.5) and he sometimes touched the inflicted part of the body, like the eyes of the two blind men (Matthew 9.29). At other times there are references to a formal laying on of hands (Mark 5.23; Luke 4.40 and 13.13). This followed Old Testament practice. There the action was regarded as a sign of spiritual blessing flowing from one person to another, as when Jacob blessed the sons of Joseph by laying his hands upon their heads (Genesis 48.8-20). The apostles followed Christ's practice when they ministered healing to others (Acts 9.12).

There is no record that Jesus used oil as a sign of healing. Perhaps that would have been inappropriate since in his own person he was God's 'Anointed One', the Messiah. But the twelve whom he sent out used oil (Mark 10.13), and in James 5.14 the elders of the church were instructed to anoint the sick when they prayed for them.

Both the laying on of hands and anointing with oil have come to be used as sacramental signs in the church's liturgy — not only in the ministry of healing but also in the ministry of baptism, confirmation and ordination, especially in the Roman Catholic and Eastern Orthodox traditions.

Laying on hands when we pray for an individual can be an encouraging gesture for anyone who is ill, provided we are sure that they would welcome it. Stand slightly to one side and place your hands gently across the forehead with the little finger touching the eyebrow and the other hand at the back of the head, as if holding a rugger ball (hands on top of a head can be uncomfortable if they are pressed down). If others are joining in the prayer, let them touch the shoulder or hold the hand of the one being prayed for.

Oil is usually applied to the forehead with a finger making the sign of the cross.

There are no hard-and-fast rules about when the laying on of hands and/or anointing should or should not be used. The laying on of hands can be used in almost any situation where we feel the Lord is leading us; but the use of oil is best left to the pastoral leadership of a congregation, except in emergencies. This seems to be the pattern in the New Testament, and this is how the church has traditionally interpreted that pattern in its sacramental practice.

37. What is 'inner healing'?

'Inner healing', 'the healing of memories', and 'prayer counselling' are the names given to a form of ministry which has been closely associated with the charismatic renewal.

The ministry looks back to the New Testament teaching that faith in Jesus Christ is only real when it results in a complete change of our hearts — a radical reorientation of our personalities. The process of dying to self and rising to Christ involves nothing less than that.

This radical reorientation is what Paul was referring to when he wrote, 'If you confess with your mouth, "Jesus is Lord," and you believe in your heart that God raised him from the dead, you will be saved. For it is with your heart that you believe and are justified, and it is with your mouth that you confess and are saved' (Romans 10.9-10).

Those who have been set in a right relationship with God through repentance and faith in Jesus Christ will be saved (made whole, healed), because what they confess will not be a verbal claim with no substance in it, but an expression of their total surrender to God from the innermost depths of their being.

As we go through life we discover from time to time areas of our personalities which are not dying to self and rising to Christ. Sometimes this will be because we are not yet willing to surrender ourselves to God in those areas; what we need to do then is ask the Lord to help us make a greater commitment of ourselves to him.

But sometimes we may not be able to make that surrender because our wills are hindered by a psychological blockage. For example, women and men who have had bad experiences in early childhood, like being deserted or ill-treated by a parent, frequently have difficulty in accepting God as their loving Father. The earlier experience has created a psychological blockage which prevents them entering into the freedom of the daughters and sons of God.

When this kind of thing occurs, such people usually require counselling to enable them to realise for themselves where the blockage in them is. Then, at an appropriate moment, prayer is offered for the healing of those circumstances which caused the emotional hurts. In the case of desertion or ill-treatment by parents, this may involve going back in the imagination to understand what caused the parents to behave in that fashion and to forgive them in the name of Jesus Christ.

In this ministry, gifts of the Spirit such as words of knowledge and discernment can play an important part. During prayer a counsellor may be given a picture, a verse of scripture or words to repeat which act as a key to unlocking hidden memories relevant to the psychological blockage. It is this aspect of the charismatic renewal which relates to this ministry.

When such blockages have been exposed and made the subject of prayer, their effects often vanish in the life of the one affected deeply by them, and they experience the peace and joy which 'inner healing' brings.

38. Does it mean I lack faith, if I go to a doctor after I have received prayer for healing?

The natural gifts exercised in the healing of people, from the body's own resources to the wonderful results of medical science and nursing care, are from God. They are his creation. Consequently when we see others involved in caring for and curing the sick, we should acknowledge that they, too, are agents of the Lord's healing, even if some of them do not personally recognise it. 'Honour the physician with the honour due to him, according to your need, for the Lord created him; for healing comes from the most High.... The Lord created medicines from the earth, and a sensible man will not despise them' (Ecclesiasticus 38.1-2,4).

It is therefore certainly not a sign of a lack of faith to consult a doctor. Indeed, we should ask those who pray with us for healing to include him in their prayers.

Furthermore, we should respect his opinion. I don't mean we should always let his opinion limit our hope in what the Lord might do. By its very nature, medical science has to abide by the results of its own research and experience. It cannot take into account acts of God's sovereign will beyond what is regarded as scientifically feasible.

A man and wife who were both general practitioners were intrigued when their Anglican vicar introduced a service of prayer for healing occasionally into their parish's Sunday programme. After a while they had a long discussion with him about the ministry of healing and asked him to teach them how to pray for people with the laying on of hands. This he did, training a few others as well. Those who received this ministry reported that the hands of the doctors on their heads felt very different from the hands of the others. They sensed a special gift of healing through them.

Respect for a patient's doctor also means that we should be careful when we talk about healings when there is no medical evidence to support those claims. We do not honour God when we say someone has been healed when no real cure has taken place. It is more honest to report that someone we have prayed with was 'feeling better' or 'showing signs of improvement'.

But, on the other hand, medical science and nursing care do not have answers to all physical, mental and emotional disorders. Sicknesses springing from spiritual troubles can only be dealt with by those who act with the Lord's spiritual authority. And if only a physical cure is effected, leaving other areas of a person's life in an unhealthy state, then the healing is incomplete. God's healing is total — in body, mind and spirit. A good test of any treatment is to ask the question, Does it help the sick person towards the recovery of a life in which he is able to grow in the love and service of God and of others?

39. Is there a difference between gifts of healing and a ministry of healing?

A gift of healing is one of the spiritual gifts listed by Paul in 1 Corinthians 12 (verses 9, 28 and 30). He spoke of the charism in the plural, 'gifts of healings', suggesting different kinds of illnesses and different ways in which God heals them.

Gifts of healing were an important feature in the ministry of Jesus Christ. Nearly one-fifth of the text of the gospels is concerned with healings. Taking into account the parallel passages in the synoptic gospels, Jesus exercised gifts of healing on forty-one occasions, including eight among 'multitudes'. These healings included three resurrections — Jairus' daughter (Mark 8.41 and parallels), the widow's son at Nain (Luke 7.11) and Lazarus (John 11.1).

Jesus' healing work was a manifestation of his saving ministry. In the New Testament there is no sharp distinction between the forgiveness of sins, the healing of sickness, and the casting out of demons. They are all 'signs' of the salvation, the wholeness, which Jesus brings us through his passion, death and resurrection. He spoke of himself as a physician: 'It is not the healthy who need a doctor, but the sick. I have not come to call the righteous, but sinners' (Mark 2.17).

Then he sent his disciples out, commissioning them to pronounce the kingdom of God and to heal. During his earthly ministry he dispatched the Twelve and the Seventy on this mission (Mark 3.13-19 and parallels, and Luke 1.24). After Pentecost the New Testament church continued Christ's healing ministry in Jesus' name by the power of the Holy Spirit.

The healing of the crippled beggar at the temple gate called Beautiful set the pattern. The man was asking for alms, but Peter had another gift for him: 'Silver or gold I do not have, but what I have I give you. In the name of Jesus Christ of Nazareth, walk' (Acts 3.6). The words indicated that the apostle did not perform the healing through his own power but by the authority of the Messiah. Further gifts of healing were manifested as the story of the New Testament church unfolded. The experience was summed up in the last verse of Mark's Gospel: 'The disciples went out and preached everywhere, and the Lord worked with them and confirmed his word by the signs that accompanied it' (Mark 16.20).

A gift of healing, then, is a sovereign act of God's grace, offered through the church by the power of the Holy Spirit in the name of Jesus Christ.

A ministry of healing is a 'service' (that is what 'ministry' means) by those who in obedience to the Spirit exercise gifts of healing as members of the church.

Because of who he was and what he was, it was not possible for Jesus to act except in dependence on his heavenly Father. 'I tell you the truth, the Son can do nothing by himself; he can only do what he sees his Father doing, because whatever the Father does the Son also does' (John 5.19). Through their union with Christ, the servants of God must do the same — in the ministry of healing as in every other ministry.

In recent years the denominations have revised their services for the sick with a stronger emphasis on the ministry of healing. These services include prayers with the laying on of hands and anointing. We see the beginnings of a more formal ministry to the sick in James 5.13-16, where the elders of the church take the initiative. This passage has been the basis for modern revisions. In present-day church services at which the ministry of healing is offered, a lead is taken by vicars and pastors ('elders'), especially in the anointing of the sick.

40. Why are some not healed after they have received the ministry of prayer?

There is no answer to this question. But the scriptures offer us certain pointers towards an answer.

The central message of the Gospel is that we are saved by the blood of Jesus Christ (Acts 20.28; Romans 3.25). As this message is proclaimed, and as women and men respond to it, God's salvation is brought to them (Romans 10.8, 14ff). The ministry of healing is within the orbit of this saving work. We need to remember that our prayers for healing are offered at the foot of the cross.

Since sickness, with sin, is evidence of the power of evil, then healing, with forgiveness, is evidence of Christ's triumph over that evil. This triumph was unfolded through Jesus' earthly ministry, particularly in the healings he bestowed on those with diseases and the liberations he brought to those who were possessed by demons. That ministry reached its victorious climax in his death and resurrection (1 Corinthians 15.20-28).

But healings are not a guaranteed by-product for all those who turn to Jesus Christ in repentance and faith. We can be no more certain that we shall be completely healthy than that we shall be completely sinless. Yet we believe that when we have repented our sins, confessed Jesus Christ as our Saviour and Lord, been baptised, and received the Holy Spirit,

then we are to count ourselves dead to sin but alive
to God in Christ Jesus (Romans 6.11).

Apply this to those apparently unanswered
prayers. Living in a sinful world we know that, even
though God does not will us to suffer, suffering and
death are inevitable for all of us. What the Father
offers us through his Spirit is communion with his
Son in his suffering and in his victory.

'We always carry around in our body the death of
Jesus, so that the life of Jesus may also be revealed
in our body. For we who are alive are always being
given over to death for Jesus' sake, so that his life
may be revealed in our mortal body' (2 Corinthians
4.10-11). Paul was writing of what he suffered as an
apostle of Jesus Christ — the preaching of the
gospel involved him in dangers and persecutions.
But the same principle applies to those who suffer
through illness: that suffering, too, can reveal the
life of Christ when it is transfigured by God's grace.

Sometimes it takes the form of a miraculous
triumph over continual pain and disability, so that
the power of the Holy Spirit in the sufferer points
others to Jesus Christ. At other times it is manifested through a faith in God which leads to a
peaceful death.

The cross shows us that God is on the side of
those who suffer and die. He is not detached from
the questions we ask about suffering which persists
after we have prayed for healing. We read in the
gospels the prayer of Christ in Gethsemane. Jesus
asked that he might not have to face the cross, but
he was willing to submit to that awful death if his
acceptance of it fulfilled the ultimate purposes of his
Father's will for the salvation of mankind.

So we pray in faith for healing, not knowing why
God allows suffering. We accept that by praying we

are involving ourselves in the mystery of God's saving purposes for us, and that often we are in the dark about how those purposes are being worked out.

Of course, it is wonderful if some miraculous healing takes place and a relative or friend is released from pain and disability. It brings a glorious glimpse of God's kingdom breaking through into our lives. But that kingdom can also break through gloriously if we ask the Holy Spirit to help us to accept whatever happens to us in the faith that God is still in control.

The Father loves us, and he wills the best for us. In one sense we all need healing always, because none of us is yet perfect in his sight. But in another sense the healing we need has already been accomplished in Jesus Christ, who died for us and included every need of ours in what he did.

That is why we can thank God in our prayers for healing. Indeed, all intercessory prayer, like all Christian living, should begin and end in praise: 'Whatever you do, whether in word or deed, do it all in the name of the Lord Jesus Christ, giving thanks to God the Father through him' (Colossians 3.17). Even when the answers to our prayers do not immediately seem to be what we had hoped for, we can still praise him.

Thanksgiving is an expression of our faith in him: 'Through Jesus, therefore, let us continually offer to God a sacrifice of praise — the fruit of lips that confess his name' (Hebrews 13.15). Deep in the heart of Christian prayer, whatever our circumstances, is the joy and peace which is the sign of the Spirit's indwelling.

One final note. There is an idea around in some Christian circles that gifts of healing depend on the

amount of faith we have and on the words we use.
So when they have prayed for the sick, people ask:
'Do you think I said the right thing?' — 'Would he
have got better quicker if I'd left out, "If it be your
will, Lord"?'

What matters in the ministry of prayer for
healing is what God does. Our role in that ministry
— as those who pray with others as well as those for
whom prayers are offered — is to trust him and to
co-operate obediently with him. We say with Job: 'I
know that you can do all things; no plan of yours
can be thwarted' (Job 42.2).

41. Is the ministry of healing the same as faith healing?

'Faith healing' is a term used very loosely for a
variety of things. It has been used of the church's
care of the sick, but this is a misleading title. It
tends to reinforce the mistake which many make
about the nature of faith and its role in the ministry
of healing. This is reflected in the things Christians
sometimes say: 'I don't have enough faith to pray
with anyone for healing,' or 'Would he have got
better if he'd had more faith?'

In all forms of medical care we have to trust —
trust in the doctor, trust in those who look after us.
But faith in God is more than trust. It is better
expressed as throwing ourselves forward into his
care and under his lordship for everything in our
lives, including our healing.

It is noteworthy that Jesus healed some who
apparently did not have any particular faith in him
at all — eg, the centurion's servant (Matthew 8.5).
It was their friends or relatives who had sufficient
faith to approach the Lord on behalf of the sick, as

in the case of the paralysed man (Mark 2.3). Others, like the woman with the haemorrhage, believed that he could cure them (Mark 5.25).

Although to some Jesus said, 'Your faith has saved you,' that did not imply that faith was always necessary in the sick person for healing. Indeed, in all the stories of Christ's healings, only seven of those he healed are said to have had faith in him. It was a general acceptance of Jesus and his message in the people around the sick which was important (though even in Nazareth, where there was little faith in him, he still healed a few sick folk, Mark 6.5).

It is for this reason that Christians are wary of using the term 'faith healing', especially since it is applied to all kinds of non-medical ministrations which have no Christian intention whatever.

A small number of people seem to have natural powers which promote healing. A woman was allowed by a hospital to use a room one day a week so that patients could consult her. She talked to them and then in silence laid her hands on their heads. It was evidently considered beneficial because she was allowed to do this for several years. Others have a more religious approach and invoke the 'healing spirits of nature'. Spiritualists also practise this.

It has to be said that, from a Christian view-point, these kinds of 'faith healings' expose the patient and those who minister to them to grave dangers. Anything undertaken outside God's covenant through Jesus Christ is open to evil influences. Without the protection of the cross, we can be lost in a spiritual vacuum. Jesus' story about the evil spirit which took seven other spirits to the clean, empty house taught that important lesson (Luke

11.24–26).

Does that mean that all 'faith healings' performed outside the Christian ministry are suspect? Some 'faith healings' may be beneficial. If in the long run the patient shows signs of an overall improvement, not only physically but inwardly as well (and it takes time to discover this), then perhaps we can believe that the Holy Spirit has been active through the ministrations the patient has received.

But many 'faith healings' do not turn out that way. There can be improvements in a patient's condition, but often the improvement is only temporary. Either the trouble recurs, or the outcome of what the patient experienced is an unhappy one.

We must take account of three considerations:

1. The devil is above all a deceiver. In his sayings about the tree and its fruit, Jesus told his disciples about the judgement on the last day: 'Many will say to me, "Lord, Lord, did we not prophesy in your name, and in your name drive out demons and perform many miracles?" Then I will tell them plainly, "I never knew you. Away from me, you evil-doers."' (Matthew 7.22-23). If Jesus can condemn as evil some of the miraculous works performed in his name, what can we decide about healings which are performed without reference to his name?

2. The only true healing is that which brings us to a deeper repentance and faith in Jesus Christ. Anything less than that is not the true healing which God offers us. It is something less.

3. By submitting ourselves to the ministrations of a 'faith healer' (no matter how well-intentioned she or he might be), we are inevitably looking to

someone or something else for healing — to a spirit of natural healing, or to a person with strange healing powers. And when we do such things, we run the risk of worshipping other gods. That is the great apostasy about which the scriptures make many severe warnings.

RENEWAL IN THE CONGREGATION

42. How does a local congregation respond to the charismatic renewal?

I will list below some of the responses made by the pastor, lay leaders and members when as a congregation they seek to be renewed charismatically by the Holy Spirit. Obviously these responses will vary from one place to another, and from one denomination to another; but certain common results are often discerned.

1. Individual members of the congregation begin to respond at a greater depth to the life in the Spirit.

They are more aware of God as Father and Judge, of Jesus as Saviour and Brother, and of the Holy Spirit as God present in power, especially in spiritual gifts. They are also more aware of the spiritual warfare in which they are involved.

2. They become more conscious of belonging to 'the Body of Christ', a description of the church which comes to have more meaning for them.

Sensitivity to the Spirit brings a sensitivity towards other Christians. Although this begins in the congregation, it overflows the denominational boundaries as the members of other traditions are seen more as fellow Christians with spiritual gifts and ministries. This is noticeable in neighbourhoods where councils of churches and other ecumenical projects have for years survived with a minimum of commitment. In my job as an ecumenical officer, I have noticed such councils and projects taking on a strikingly new and vigorous lease of life when charismatics get involved in them.

3. There is a slow but radical change from the static, vicar/pastor-orientated kind of church life to a more dynamic concept of ministry.

The practical effect of this is that the vicar/pastor

becomes an 'overseer' or 'leader of leaders' as he learns to share his eldership with other mature women and men in the congregation, who may or may not be given the title of 'elders'. Church council meetings and the like usually become 'deacons, meetings', mainly concerned with finance and practical administration. The 'elders' meet, pray and discuss matters of pastoral care and strategy. It is this development which causes tensions in denominations where the traditional structures are not designed to encourage such forms of active 'diaconate' and 'eldership'.

4. Larger congregations are usually broken down into smaller house groups.

Leaders are appointed who exercise pastoral care over these groups. It is within this small cell that the members minister to one another and grow in spiritual maturity. The group leaders in their turn become a pastoral group presided over either by the vicar/pastor himself or by the eldership of the congregation.

5. Other gifted ministries are recognised in the congregation, such as administration, prophecy, healing, and so on.

Individuals are often surprised at the way the Holy Spirit leads them to serve the congregation or the neighbourhood. Counselling, evangelism and music are ministries which are frequently developed by individuals and groups, especially in those local congregations where these have been neglected. The ideal set before the congregation is that every member should be a functioning part of the local body of believers.

6. Healing (including counselling) becomes an important part of the congregation's programme.

This ministry is offered at the main Sunday service or sometimes at a special service of prayer for healing, as well as in homes and hospitals.

7. *Training and teaching become more central to the congregation's life.*

This is not done by the vicar/pastor alone but by the other gifted individuals. There is a growing tendency for congregations with their leaders to minister to one another — the pastor and a team from one congregation visiting and sharing with another.

8. *Planned giving rises above other money-making efforts as the major source of the congregation's income.*

In many places the 'tithe' (one-tenth of a household's disposable income) is accepted as a standard to be aimed at. The greater availability of funds allows for an expansion of pastoral work in areas such as community care schemes and support of missionary and other important ministries out-side the congregation. In some places the congrega-tion is able to sponsor a gifted individual in a full-time ministry such as that of an evangelist or a counsellor.

9. *Joyous, spontaneous worship and the flow of the gifts of the Spirit are infused either into the regular worshipping tradition of the church or into special prayer and praise meetings on Sunday evenings or midweek.*

10. *The renewed congregation seeks to share its life with other local churches, and united missions of all kinds are initiated in the neighbourhood.*

Joint 'celebrations' are frequently held. There is more social concern and outreach — by individuals as well as by groups. Church planting — starting a new congregation with a core group from the old one — is another development. The leaders of a group of congregations seeking renewal in the Spirit often form a ministers' fellowship in which they support and encourage one another.

43. Is charismatic worship different from ordinary worship in a church?

We can only offer ourselves, our souls and bodies to God if the Holy Spirit moves through our congregation to stir us and equip us with his gifts (charisms) for worship. In the strictest theological sense, then, all church services are charismatic (gifted) if they are to be authentic acts of worship. That is why at the beginning of most services there is a prayer invoking God's Spirit on the congregation. Since we are often lukewarm in our faith, we need his renewing grace within our lives to make our worship real before him.

Worship is not made more charismatic because participants lift their hands in the air and sing choruses. Renewed worship will only come from a body of Christians who have faith in the renewing power of God in their lives and who are growing in love towards one another in Jesus Christ.

What the signs of this will be is difficult to specify because congregations and their liturgical traditions vary so much.

The quiet chanting of the psalms and the attention given to the scripture readings and prayers in a Roman Catholic community of monks or nuns can be a Spirit-filled experience of worship for the participants because of the quality of their commitment to one another and their inherited customs. But to a visitor who is unfamiliar both with the community and with that form of liturgy, it can seem formal and impersonal — though a discerning visitor will realise this is a renewing act of worship when he finds himself responding to the movement of the Spirit in that community.

Noisy Pentecostal worship with much chorus-singing, clapping and shouting of 'Alleluias' might well be off-putting to a Christian who is used to a formal liturgy with controlled ceremonial. But the visitor might discover in that Pentecostal congregation a deep love of the Lord and an eager desire to serve him in one another — and that discovery might well alter his attitude towards the type of worship he experiences among them.

There is often more feeling — individual as well as corporate — in the worship of a charismatic congregation. This is expressed not only in the spirit of the singing and praying but also in the way members sway their bodies, lift their hands, and look at one another during, say, the singing of a chorus.

But basically there are certain things which help a congregation to be more charismatic in their worship (whether they think of themselves as 'charismatics' or not).

1. An attitude of expectant faith that God will speak to them and equip them for their Christian discipleship. I don't mean that everyone should arrive at the church door in a high state of excited belief, or that individuals should stifle their doubts and questionings. I mean that, from the leadership outwards, there should be a sense of quiet anticipation that the Lord is present and that he is going to move among them.

This attitude is not arrived at suddenly. It requires months of careful teaching and prayer by the leadership so that there emerges in the congregation a willingness to engage in the mission of God's kingdom. The members themselves need to be built up as a community in Jesus Christ and to serve God by the power of the Spirit in the society of which they are a part. It is when this becomes an

experience for many of them that they approach
worship with expectant faith.

2. A pastoral leadership which is united in its
obedience to God. Leadership in the body of Christ
is always a collaborative affair. Even if a congregation only has one vicar/pastor, he or she will be
learning to share that leadership with others in the
congregation, who have the appropriate gifts for
this ministry.

If the pastor allows his own personal difficulties
to triumph without invoking the grace of God to
cope with them, then the way he approaches
worship will affect the whole congregation. This
doesn't mean a pastor can only take a service when
he is free of personal difficulties. What it means is
that one who is not relying on God to deal with the
problems in his own life will dampen the renewing
Spirit in the worship he leads. The congregation
will sense the difference between the pastor who is
still struggling in the Spirit and the one who has
abandoned hope of God's aid.

3. This leads into the third factor — the
orderliness of the worship. The pastor should be
open to the Spirit who will equip him to lead that
congregation on that occasion with opportunities
for participation as appropriate. This is where the
use of different spiritual gifts comes in. He will
encourage individuals and groups in the congregation to share with the rest, and control what is
disruptive or exhibitionist.

To assist him — indeed, to free him in his
response to the Spirit — is the liturgy, the
framework around which the act of worship is built.
Within its ordered progress the pastor incorporates
what is spontaneous and local as he discerns the
Spirit's leading. Some of the most memorable and

inspiring acts of worship I have attended have been those led within a traditional structure, such as an Anglican evensong or a Roman Catholic eucharist.

4. These traditional structures ensure that the worship grows out of the scriptures. They provide for readings from the Bible and prayers incorporating scriptural material. But they require hymns and songs which enable the congregation to affirm their faith and to praise the Lord within the unfolding theme of the service. What is provided in the liturgical material should point worshippers to the highest aspirations which the scriptures offer us for our discipleship and destiny in Jesus Christ.

5. Out of the biblical material used in worship there is also a proclamation of the Word of God. Generally this is in the form of a sermon; but other means of proclaiming the Word are used sometimes — gently sung choruses of scriptural passages, simple dramatic presentations, visual and audio aids of different kinds. Within this proclamation the testimonies of individuals are occasionally made.

6. There may sometimes be a manifestation of the spiritual gifts especially associated with the charismatic renewal — a prophecy or a word of knowledge, a gift of tongues followed by an interpretation, a ministry of healing offered unobtrusively during the service. These do not necessarily mean that the worship becomes more charismatic; but when the Lord's word is heard and his grace is seen through such manifestations during a church service, it is powerfully encouraging to the worshippers.

7. Behind this worship, of course, will be the life and ministry of the congregation. As I have already said, no techniques can renew the worship of a congregation if its members are not growing in their

awareness of God's grace in their daily lives.

44. Why are charismatics always saying 'Praise the Lord!' and raising their hands in the air?

I feel uneasy, too, when I'm with a charismatic who says 'Praise the Lord!' on every conceivable occasion. It cheapens what is intended to be something very precious (like those bus conductors in London who call their passengers 'darling'!).

'Praise the Lord!' is the recognition that, as Christ's church, we should be a praising and thankful people. We are not to take all that God has done for granted. 'Give thanks in all circumstances, for this is God's will for you in Christ Jesus' (1 Thessalonians 5.18).

This thankfulness springs from the faith that, no matter what we are going through, God is always loving and forgiving. If we can embrace that faith effectively with our hearts as well as intellectually with our minds, it will enable us to see things more in the light of God's will rather than of our own expectations or fears.

But praise must be honest; it must spring from self-knowledge. There's no place for trying to boost our morale through our own efforts, or for trying to deceive ourselves or others. That's another danger of using 'Praise the Lord!' too casually. When praise truly comes from our hearts, it will lift us above our circumstances, whatever we happen to be feeling.

The author of Hebrews urged his readers to be a people who praise God: 'Through Jesus, therefore, let us continually offer to God a sacrifice of praise — the fruit of lips that confess his name' (Hebrews

13.15). There will be times when we focus our attention on the Lord, forgetting about ourselves and joining with others in praise. This is a characteristic of charismatic worship which some Christians find difficult to appreciate. They are uneasy that a crowd of worshippers should spend so much time singing choruses of devotion in a free-wheeling manner. They are even more uneasy when the crowd makes a cheerful noise unto the Lord and shouts for joy! It is often a temperamental or a cultural stumbling-block that causes this.

Then there will be times when we focus our attention on the Lord in silence, perhaps after reading a psalm or a passage of scripture and express our thanksgiving inwardly to him. In our thanksgiving we are responding to all that the Lord has done for us. In our praise we are acknowledging who he is in all his glory. And, as we do this, we realise once more that he is Lord, that his ways are not our ways, that we must be obedient to him if our praise is not to be false, and that we must be open to the fresh touch of his Holy Spirit.

Now the church has always encouraged her members to praise God and to give thanks to him in worship. The liturgy is full of praise. Words such as, 'Glory be to the Father, and to the Son, and to the Holy Spirit' are repeated often. At every eucharist this (or something like it) is proclaimed, 'It is right at all times and in all places to give you thanks and praise, holy Father.' The most popular hymns are those which praise God.

But much of this praise is formal. Many Christians seem to have lost the prayer of praise in their devotions, or they have not realised what they can thank God for in their daily lives. Renewal in the Holy Spirit brings with it a renewal in praise and reveals how much we have to thank God for. When they discover this — through the charismatic renewal or through anything which helps them to be more open to the Spirit — Christians instinctively want to praise God more.

In the exuberance of their new discovery, charismatics at first probably overdo it. So we have to be sure that when we say 'Praise the Lord!' it comes from our hearts as a response to all that God has done for us. And if we make praise an important part of our worship, we shall not only be following the best traditions of Christian liturgy; we shall also find that God is changing our lives and sending us out to others in his love and power.

Lifting up hands is one of the oldest gestures known for prayer. There are many references to it in the scriptures, eg, 'I will lift up my hands towards your Most Holy Place' (Psalm 28.2).

It has remained a formal posture for prayer throughout the church's history. In some of the earliest Christian paintings in the catacombs in Rome, which date from the second and third centuries, worshippers are shown with their hands lifted up, and in more formal worship today the leader often adopts this position.

There is something psychologically satisfying in this gesture for prayers of praise and thanksgiving. It expresses openness to God, and that openness is always necessary if we are to receive all that he wishes to give us.

'I will extol the Lord at all times; his praise will be always on my lips' (Psalm 34.1).

45. What happens in a charismatic prayer group?

The difference between a charismatic prayer group and other kinds of prayer groups is that in the former there is an expectation that gifts of the Spirit such as tongues, interpretations, and prophecies will occasionally be manifested, together with words of wisdom and knowledge if there is need for informal counselling.

I don't want to imply that other kinds of prayer groups are less inspired because those who participate do not expect these particular charisms. Indeed, I've no doubt that other spiritual gifts are available in them for the teaching and encouragement of those who join them. But the charismatic prayer group has this distinction, and I want to explain why.

The charisms I have mentioned all depend on our willingness to speak aloud in faith, trusting that the Spirit will take what we say and use it for his purposes. In earlier answers in this book I have described how we can respond when we are prompted to speak in tongues or utter a simple prophecy.

These charisms also depend, however, on others being willing to listen to what we say and to discern what is of God and what is not. Otherwise the gift is not tested; nor is it 'heard' in the biblical sense of that word (that is, communicated to those for whom it is intended).

These facts underline the truth that spiritual gifts are a ministry in the church, for in order to be fruitful they have to be manifested in the fellowship of others. And a small group of Christians whom we can trust is an ideal form of that fellowship within which such testing can take place, especially in the early years of our experience of renewal.

I speak for a good many charismatics when I say that it was in such a prayer group that I first spoke in tongues before others and interpreted another's gift of tongues, laid hands on another for healing, and prayed through personal problems with the help of friends with gifts of knowledge and wisdom. It was because I could trust the group that I felt free to launch out into what was then a very unfamiliar kind of ministry. I knew that if I made mistakes — and I made many — they would understand and correct me.

The charismatic prayer group, then, begins by being a training centre for these ministries in the Spirit. It is only after we have 'experimented' (in the sense of 'become experienced') in these charisms that we become more discerning in how to use those gifts in larger gatherings. In exercising nearly all the spiritual gifts I have discussed in this book, the small group is where we can make the first responses to the Holy Spirit.

But the charismatic prayer group for some becomes more than a training cell: it also becomes a basic Christian community. By 'basic' I mean that form of Christian community where they find a reliable foundation for their own development as a disciple.

At one time these basic Christian communities were provided by the relationship which existed among extended families and neighbourhoods where people were born, grew up, married, bore children, worked, spent their leisure, grew old and died. The Christian influence of the extended family and the familiar neighbourhood was considerable in the lives of individuals. Now that society has become more mobile and impersonal, many congregations find it necessary to encourage 'extended families' among their members. These cells become 'churches-in-the-home' where individuals can be ministered to and develop their own ministries.

They are a feature of modern church life in different parts of the world today. They are not all the result of the charismatic renewal; but they are certainly signs of the Holy Spirit's creation as he equips the church for its task in contemporary society.

46. Don't charismatic prayer groups become elitist?

They can do, if the leadership in them is not watchful, and if the members of the groups are more concerned with themselves than with the rest of the congregation. An unholy huddle is the very opposite of what any Christian group should be.

On the other hand, we cannot expect a small group of Christians to grow together as the Body of Christ unless they spend some time in each other's company and unless there develops a bond of loyalty among them. It is a fact of human experience that we can only relate closely to a limited number of people at a time; and we should not expect to have the same relationships with a congregation of two hundred as we have with a group of ten or a dozen.

Charismatic groups mature through various stages. First, they come together and through a number of meetings come to understand and trust one another. Then they learn how to reflect on the word of God in the scriptures and experiment with the use of spiritual gifts. After they have become more discerning in the use of spiritual gifts, they are ready to seek what the Lord wants them to do in the wider church.

This is a crucial point in the development of the group. The leadership of the group needs the help of the pastoral leadership of the congregation to enable the group to begin to fulfil its ministry beyond its own membership. If the pastoral leadership fails the group at this point, the chances are that the group will either retreat into its own fellowship or — in the worst instances — break away from the main congregation, perhaps to form its own house church.

I have known many valuable initiatives of service and mission spring from groups of this kind. Some of the services were directed towards the congregation — in the formation of a music group, the building up of a team of counsellors, and the establishment of ecumenical enterprises with other Christian congregations. Other services were directed more towards the community — in the setting up of training schemes for the unemployed, the launching of the fund to establish a hospice, or the promotion of an evangelistic project with other Christians in the town.

Studies of the pastoral development in congregations in different parts of the world seem to show that many Christians need to experience the Christian fellowship (at least for some of their lives) in three dimensions: the cell, the congregation, and the celebration.

Most of us experience the congregation in our local churches, where any number of believers from thirty or forty to several hundreds gather for worship. We may not know them all, but they give us an awareness of what it means to be the people of God in a neighbourhood or town.

Most of us occasionally experience the celebration at big rallies or in cathedral services, where hundreds or thousands from different neighbourhoods or towns come together. Most of those participating will be strangers to us, but they give us an awareness of what it means to be the people of God in a wider area — a region or a nation.

The cell gives an awareness of what it means to be in the family of God, in which we are known for ourselves — our personalities, our needs, our spiritual gifts, and so on. Ideally, the charismatic prayer group should provide the 'cell' experience of the church.

Not all Christians will want to be in such groups, however. Some will already have their own informal cells among the friends they meet regularly in various ways. Others will be going through a stage when they want to be left alone with their natural families. These preferences should always be respected.

47. Will you explain what 'slain in the Spirit', 'heavy shepherding', and 'walking in the light' mean?

Much of this jargon has come from those nineteenth-century revivals which gave birth to the Pentecostal churches. They are examples of the cultural baggage in which some of the lessons of the charismatic renewal were delivered to us by our American friends!

Being 'slain in the Spirit' (or 'falling/resting in the Spirit') happens sometimes when an individual receives the laying on of hands while standing, usually for healing, deliverance or strengthening. He collapses to the ground and remains there for some minutes, completely relaxed and in a semi-dreamy state of consciousness. Many claim that through the experience God dealt at a deep level with them (it has been described as 'God's anaesthesia'). 'Slain' is used in the biblical sense of 'pierced'.

I don't know of any rational explanation for this phenomenon. It seems to be associated with the ministry of certain teachers, and I wonder if some of those who go forward for ministry half-expect it to happen to them — especially when 'catchers' stand behind them when they receive the laying on of hands! But this does not explain why it happens unexpectedly elsewhere. A few of the people I've prayed with have collapsed to the ground, and I certainly was not expecting that kind of reaction. It could be that during the laying on of hands the individual surrenders to the Holy Spirit to such an extent that his muscles give way causing him to fall to the ground. I have never heard of anyone hurting themselves in doing this.

'Heavy shepherding' describes the strong, authoritarian leadership exercised by certain pastors over the people in their congregation, usually through elders or group leaders. It is associated with some house churches (but by no means all). The individual member submits his life and that of his family to the guidance of the pastor or elder, even in details such as how much money to spend on a holiday or which school to send a child to.

For some individuals and families at critical moments in their lives, heavy shepherding can be beneficial — if it is wise and loving. Many marriage breakdowns would have been avoided if the couple had submitted to such pastoral oversight before their relationships were ruined. Parents facing difficulties with their children would also be helped. But sadly not all pastors and elders have the grace to discern when the heavy hand of the shepherd should be lifted to enable the individual to grow in the grace which God gives him. Stories have been circulated about the bad results of this kind of leadership so that the phrase 'heavy shepherding' has become almost a term of abuse.

'Walking in the light' (from 1 John 1.7) describes the attempt to live each day in complete openness to God and to one another. In various communities and groups touched by renewal, the members make deliberate attempts to ensure that no misunderstanding or ill-feeling comes between them.

Sometimes the practice includes confessing faults to one another. There are precedents for this throughout Christian history — as in the regular meetings in the religious orders where the members own up to any personal breaches of the community's rules, known as 'the chapter of faults'.

Obviously this kind of discipline can only be exercised among small communities and groups which have a strong sense of commitment and trust among the members.

48. What should I do if my congregation is hostile to the charismatic renewal?

They cannot be hostile to the Holy Spirit and still hope to be disciples of Jesus Christ! What is happening in the congregation is probably one of two things:

Either they have many misunderstandings of what charismatic renewal is all about, plus maybe some bad experiences which have reinforced their prejudices. Or they are moving into that state which Jesus referred to in his warnings to the Pharisees: 'These people honour me with their lips, but their hearts are far from me' (Isaiah 29.13; Matthew 15.8).

With either of these reactions there can often be a good deal of fear — fear of what the Lord might be asking them to do!

Never assume that you are in a congregation of the second kind without careful discernment and testing by others from outside as well as inside its membership. Discount that possibility and assume that, when you encounter hostility to the renewal, it is because of the first reason.

Usually these misunderstandings stem from the attitude of the pastoral leadership, so I will discuss the problem in those terms.

In dispelling these misunderstandings, much will depend on your personal attitude towards the leadership. If you give them the impression you regard them as 'second-class Christians', then you will be putting yourself in a position where you are not able to help them.

Instead, you should continue to respect them and their leadership, and be alert to the good gifts which God is giving them. I have met plenty of leaders who don't pray in tongues but who do have great charisms of pastoral love and care.

Pray that the Lord will open up for you opportunities to correct misunderstandings and to show what the Holy Spirit is offering the church today through the charismatic renewal. Avoid arguments about scriptural texts on individual charisms. Emphasise the need we all have for the Spirit's guidance and power if we are to be effective servants of God.

When it is appropriate, introduce the leadership to other charismatics — perhaps informally or by taking them to renewal meetings in the neighbourhood. If they have theological hang-ups about different aspects of the renewal, suggest they read the relevant books (you can get advice about this from the agencies I have listed in answer to the last question).

But above all, involve yourself as fully as you can in the life of the congregation. Show them that you love them and want to be with them in all that they do. It's love that counts in the end, not the most spectacular spiritual gifts. Take particular care not to be judgemental and critical. Focus your devotion and attention on Jesus, and pray every day that he will lead them with you into a more powerful witness and service in his name.

You are not being disloyal if you attend meetings and conferences on the renewal outside the congregation. Nearly all of us need encouragement and teaching from outside our own local churches, and this is quite a normal feature of Christian practice. To go to a charismatic prayer meeting in a neighbouring town, say, is no different from going to support a missionary society at its annual rally. In this way many find themselves supported in their personal search for spiritual renewal while in the midst of an unsympathetic congregation.

Is it ever right to leave a congregation and seek another in these circumstances? Yes, I think it can be — either as a last resort, or in order to protect the Christian development of the younger members of our families. But this is such a difficult judgement to make that it should be undertaken only after seeking advice from fellow Christians. And it is an obvious Christian courtesy to talk it over also with the pastoral leadership of the congregation you want to leave.

49. Do you expect every member of every congregation to become a charismatic?

If by that you mean, do I expect every member to speak in tongues and worship with their hands in the air, then the answer is, no! But if you mean, do I expect every member to be renewed in the Spirit day by day so that they exercise charisms to the glory of God and the building up of the church, then the answer is, yes!

There are other ways of being renewed in the Spirit than through the lessons of what we call the charismatic renewal. But it is the same Spirit who renews us, and in that sense I do expect every member of every congregation to become charismatic.

That expectation is summed up beautifully in the prayer used at confirmation services:

> Defend, O Lord, your servants with your heavenly grace,
> that they may continue yours for ever,
> and daily increase in your Holy Spirit more and more,
> until they come to your everlasting kingdom.

50. How can I find out more about the charismatic renewal?

In the larger denominations in Britain there are service committees which have been established by charismatics in order to inform their fellow-members what the renewal is about and how congregations and communities within their denomination are responding to God through it. These agencies publish newsletters and courses, and they organise local and national conferences.

These service committees are:

Church of England:
Anglicans for Renewal, 6 Scriven Road, Knaresborough, North Yorkshire HG5 9EQ.

Roman Catholic Church
The National Service Committee for Catholic Charismatic Renewal, 48 King's Road, London SW10 0LF.

Methodist Church:
Dunamis Renewal Fellowship, Cliff House, Calver, Sheffield, South Yorkshire S30 1XG.

United Reformed Church:
GEAR (Group for Evangelism and Renewal), 99 Norfolk Avenue, Sanderstead, South Croydon, Surrey CR2 8BY.

Certain communities run conferences regularly on various aspects of charismatic renewal. These include:

Lee Abbey, Lynton, North Devon EX35 6JJ

Scargill House, Kettlewell, Skipton, North Yorkshire BD23 5HU

Lamplugh House, Thwing, Driffield, North Humberside YO25 0DY

It is impossible to list the enormous number of books that have been published on this subject in the last twenty-five years. Many Christian book-shops have a special section on the renewal.

The monthly *Renewal* magazine, Broadway House, Broadway, Crowborough, East Sussex TN6 1BY, is a popular forum for news, articles, book reviews, and advertisements for courses and confer-ences. Send for a free sample copy.

Other Highland Books

EVANGELISM IN THE EARLY CHURCH

Michael Green

Canon Michael Green is both an evangelist and a New Testament scholar. This has enabled him to produce one of the finest books on this subject ever written.

'Expert...a most lucid examination.'

Daily Telegraph

THE HALLELUJAH FACTOR

Jack R. Taylor

The Hallelujah Factor is a treasure-house of biblical
riches which will draw the reader towards God,
starting him on a new adventure into the principles
and practice of praise.

ISBN 0 946616 18 3